Secrets of Attorney Marketing Law School Dares Not Teach

by Richard Jacobs

ISBN-13: 978-0-9894779-0-1

Warning & Disclaimer

The intent of this book is to be informational in nature only. Marketing techniques described herein may be considered to be unethical by your local or State Bar Association, or they may be prohibited due to local, state, or federal laws.

Laws change, times change, and you must do your due diligence to ensure that following any of the marketing techniques in this book will not cause you legal or tax problems, or put you in conflict with your local or state Bar association. No legal or tax advice is being given by the author, publisher, or anyone associated with this work.

Publisher, author, and all parties associated with this work are unaware of any material conflicts or issues that the implementation of these marketing techniques described herein may have or cause. This book is purely informational in nature, not to be taken as an instruction manual.

The effectiveness of the techniques described in this book cannot be guaranteed, especially if implemented improperly or half-heartedly. The techniques may boost your sales, have no effect, or even hurt your sales. The author and all parties involved in this publication take no responsibility for any outcome if you choose to use this material.

For legal advice, consult a qualified attorney. For tax advice, consult a qualified tax professional.

Copyright & Legal Notice

Richard Jacobs
Attorney Marketing Specialist
Speakeasy Marketing, Inc.
73-03 Bell Blvd #10
Oakland Gardens, N.Y. 11364
(888) 225-8594
Web: www.SpeakeasyMarketingInc.com

Client Testimonials

"I Retained 34 Clients in 2012 From My Website"

During my years of marketing companies and vendors, I have found Richard and his company to stand above the rest as being both reliable and responsive.

Being an attorney, I carefully screen who I let work with me, one of the reasons being that ethics are vital to everything I do in my practice and in maintaining my professional license.

I've watched Richard's methods and ideas become tremendously more relevant to what real attorneys need to run a successful practice. He's a valuable resource and I highly recommend his SEO, website design, and marketing services to serious attorneys."

Kevin Leckerman, Esq.
(South New Jersey / Eastern Pennsylvania)
www.LeckermanLaw.com

"The Past 2 Months Were The Busiest I've Had In Years."

"Like most attorneys, I was highly skeptical and resistant to trying direct mail to attract new clients.

It took a good deal of urging from Richard Jacobs to get me to dip my toe in the water and try it out, mainly because I thought it was an unprofessional and undignifed way to attract clients.

After all, I've been practicing for over 20 years and didn't think this method of marketing would work, nor that I needed it.

Turns out, after just 1 month of doing a very small initial test run, I retained 3 new clients and a huge ROI on the money I spent.

Carl Spector, Esq.
www.NJ-CriminalAttorneys.com

....

"Website completely redesigned in 30 Days. Helped me author 2 books (DUI / Traffic) –I'm impressed."

"Richard Jacobs started out providing me DUI and traffic ticket leads, and I then hired him to re-design my website and do SEO work for me.

Without delay, Richard jumped on the task, designed and made live a new website for me in less than a month, helped me author 2 books (one on DUI, one on traffic offenses), and set up phone and email tracking of leads.

I have been very impressed by his work and speed of delivery, and I would recommend his attorney-marketing services to other attorneys, without hesitation."

Mark J. Bigger, Esq.
www.MarkBigger.com

"Richard has a very astute sense of what's working, and it's not always the quick fix."

"Richard has a very astute sense as to what is working, not always easy, or the quick fix lawyers are looking for, but that if you take that approach which is providing value, you'll reap many times the value.

In my experience, providing good, high quality content, and a thoughtful approach to marketing is one that I really appreciate from him."

Seth Price, Esq.
www.PriceBenowitz.com

"Always Answers My Calls. Fantastic Service. A Friend and Trusted Advisor."

I've been working with Speakeasy Marketing and Richard Jacobs for over a year. In the beginning, I was highly skeptical that any of his DUI leads would pan out, but I quickly saw that Richard is for real and his work is top notch.

Rich has helped me write a book on Military DUI, created a new website that far exceeds my previous one, and has been instrumental in helping me attract and retain more clients. I highly recommend his services to any attorney who is serious about improving his practice and making more money.

Shannon I. Wilson, Esq.
www.BridgetownLaw.com

TABLE OF CONTENTS(1 of 3)

TABLE OF CONTENTS(2 of 3)

TABLE OF CONTENTS(3 of 3)

Introduction: I Didn't Write A Single Word Of This Book... (huh?)

Right off the bat, I have a confession to make. I didn't write a single word of this book. How is that possible? Well, I didn't have a ghostwriter write it, nor did I write it myself.

Actually, I spoke it. I sat in front of my computer, used some crib notes, spoke to the screen, recorded my voice, and had it transcribed; then I editeditto take out the "um's", "uh's", "duh's", and badly spoken sentences. That's why I say I spoke, not wrote this book.

Later I will reveal to my attorney readers out there, why speaking a book (as opposed to "old fashioned writing") is a big time breakthrough you can use in **your own practice**.

Who Is Richard Jacobs, Attorney Marketing Specialist, and Frankly, Who Cares?

So who am I, and why did I speak this book? Why should you read or believe anything I have to say? My name is Richard Jacobs, and I've been doing online and offline marketing for criminal defense attorneys for the past 3 plus years now.

As you can see by the testimonials in this book, I know what I am doing. I've gotten real results for real attorneys. Anyone reading is welcome to call these guys and gals and ask about my work. They''ll give you an honest assessment.

How did I get into the legal field, consulting with attorneys when I am not an attorney myself? Here's my history:

One night, about three and a half years ago, I was surfing the web, possibly drinking a beer or two, and I decided to look up the most expensive Google Pay Per Click keywords out there. I learned "DUI lawyer" and "mesothelioma lawyer" were some of the most expensive keywords, running anywhere from $30 to $100 per click.

I figured, "Hmm, this is a market that should have some money in it because it looks like people are spending a whole heck of a lot on advertising." I wondered; do I want to deal with attorneys? They're kind of a mean, scary bunch... but I deliberately chose to throw myself into it, not only for the potential money, but for the big challenge.

My thinking at the time was: If I can use SEO (search engine optimization) to be number 1 in Google for terms like "Los Angeles DUI lawyer" or "New York DWI attorney"- and not have to pay $50 or $60 per click that some people appeared to be paying, then I might be able to make a pretty substantial business out of this.

So initially I started myDuiAttorney.org, providing advertising to attorneys nationwide to help them get DUI / DWI leads.

The site obviously started with zero visitors, and from scratch, I built it up to well over 1,000 visitors a day from Google. It took a year and a half to do it, but I did it. At its peak, I had 120 attorney clients, all paying for advertising.

After doing that for a while, I grew discouraged because I realized I was a one trick pony. Here I was providing leads to attorneys, but some attorneys were great at converting leads to retained clients, while others were god-awful and couldn't convert to save their lives.

Also, sometimes leads would go dry in a particular city or metrofor 2 weeks or more, and attorneys would freak out and quit the service.

With so many clients, I had no relationship with them. The only time they called or emailed was to complain or quit. I decided I didn't want to operate like that and live in fear of my clients calling me to complain.

I wanted to work more closely with attorneys and help them market their practice, no matter if that meant getting online leads, doing direct mail, Yellow Pages, or a combination of several marketing methods.

So I cannibalized that entire business and sold the website. I slimmed down to about 25 attorney clients, and now I talk to my clients about every two weeks and have a much closer relationship with them. We spend a lot of time talking about what's working and what is not. In the past year and a half, I have had to learn all about how attorneys practice; all the different ways they can market themselves; what works and what doesn't and I'm a much better marketer because of it!

Some of the topics I am going to talk about in this book are: SEO, the good and the bad; and why page one of Google is actually a meaningless waste of time. I am going to talk about direct mail, which is called a "jailer mailer" in some places. I am going to talk about increasing your authority and celebrity by authoring your own book; specifically by speaking it rather than procrastinating about writing for 5-10 years and still never getting it done. (sound familiar?)

You'll read about Google pay-per-click, getting referrals from past clients and how to increase referrals; how to build an effective website that actually gets people interested in your message and compels them to call you, not just visit your site and leave 2 seconds later without spending quality time reading and getting educated about their legal issues from your articles, blogs, and content.

We'll go over testing and tracking all your results and why that is critical in order not to be an advertising victim; you'll learn how to spot bad actors out there that take all your money and leave you with nothing; all under the guise of marketing your practice for you.

With this in mind, I welcome you inside this book. You'll likely find it contrarian, abrasive, massively useful, straight to the point with zero fluff, and above all, an eye-opener.

...Now open your mind and let's begin:

Screw Professionalism - Having an Open Mind

I'm not afraid to tell you every detail of how I help attorneys market their practice, and you'll soon see that I'm not kidding, either. Why am I not afraid? Don't I have "trade secrets" to protect?

In my experience, 95% of all the people I give advice to don't follow it. They say, "Yeah that sounds good" or "I don't think that will work", or "That's unprofessional", **and they do nothing.**

I am not worried about competition, nor am I worried about you knowing all my secrets. I know 95% of you, maybe even more than that, are not going to do anything I tell you in this book. Not a damn thing. So why not tell you everything, without fear, for the benefit of the few that will actually take action?

Since I'm not afraid to "reveal all", you, in turn, must keep an open mind while reading this book. Don't get hung up on thoughts such as, "That's not professional" or "People don't read nowadays." These assumptions hold you back and close your mind off to what is possible and limit your success.

Don't let anyone's opinion stop you from trying a particular kind of advertising; only reality and actual experience should be your guide.

Your gut reaction to a particular marketing method may be, "Oh, direct mail, that's unprofessional. I feel like I am hounding people by doing that." Or you might think: "Pay-per-click? It's a scam. I would never do that."

Open your mind and try this stuff. If not, you're going to remain where you are; fighting every month to cover your monthly nut and not getting ahead of the game.

...and if you DO harness your marketing and implement various marketing methods and course-correct along the way? You can make well beyond what you are making. If you want to make $400,000 a year or more as a criminal defense lawyer, IT IS POSSIBLE.

You can bring home more than you are now bringing home, but you've got to be into marketing and spend time learning and implementing it. It cannot be a done-for-you service that you never think about or interact with like the janitorial service that cleans your office after hours.

Marketing must be on your mind. It has to be a critical part of your practice. So if you're willing to have an open mind, continue reading. If not, put this book down or close out the screen and don't read any further.

YOU MAY HARBOR ASSUMPTIONS YOU DON'T EVEN KNOW YOU HAVE

As an attorney you're probably great at digging deep and uprooting assumptions in a client's case, to help them win; it's the heart of what makes you a good attorney. BUT... we're all human and have assumptions that can really hurt when it comes to marketing your practice effectively.

Here are some of the most <u>Poisonous Assumptions</u> I hear on a daily basis:

"My clients are different. They are sophisticated, white collar people who wouldn't respond to this kind of marketing."

"My clients are different. They are unsophisticated, blue collar folks who don't read. They don't have patience for this kind of stuff."

"Direct mail is unethical. I just don't want to do it. You only get cheapskate tire-kickers, anyway."

"My competitor, Joe Blow, Esq., is at the top of page 1 of Google for 'Timbuktu criminal defense lawyer,' or 'Dallas DWI attorney', so he must be doing really well. If I could justget above him in Google, THAT would solve all my problems."

"I've been a lawyer for 25 years, son. Do you think anything you tell me, I haven't heard or tried before? Please."

"The economy is really bad. People have no money. That's just how it is."

"Everyone's on a payment plan. No one has money to pay. In this economy people are barely surviving as it is, so how can I afford to do marketing?"

Once your mind has accepted these assumptions as true, you are essentially throwing a wet blanket over your ability to market. These assumptions are Pure Poison.

When I worked in the DUI arena as a provider of group attorney advertising, would you like to know some of the myriad things I tried, marketing-wise that either succeeded or failed?

I made custom coasters, matchbooks, wristbands and napkins with a call to action to call (800) 555-5555 if you are arrested for a DUI.

I got the agreement of 50+ local bars around the country to hand them out to customers, place beneath their drinks, and use in their bar because I provided these items, free.

Although I didn't get a ton of calls, people did call that were actually arrested for DUI and attorneys got clients because of the advertising. Would you imagine such a way of advertising would work? Can't know until you try.

I've done direct mailings. One was a crumpled letter inside a mini trash can, offering legal assistance to potential clients. We did this for an attorney for their direct mail package.

Guess what? It generated a lot of calls who actually became clients of my attorney (and paid him!). Why? Because it was crazy and unique to receive a trash can in the mail, vs. a boring letter inside a boring, white envelope, with the same boring gobbledygook every other attorney sends.

I have also written & emailed, to tens of thousands of website visitors, a 7-part email series called an email auto-responder.

Once someone fills in a form on the web to request help with a DUI charge, it automatically started emailing step 1, then 2, 3, 4 etc. to the person that inquired every 3 days.

Each email gave an explanation of some aspect of DUI that was educational in nature, not a sales pitch. As a result, people called back. They came back from the abyss of the internet to call, and even retain some of the attorneys who advertised on the site.

What other crazy marketing schemes have I tried?

I've interviewed well over 126 attorneys over Skype and phone. (ofcourse the video quality was unprofessional and not the best, and so were the questions I asked).

I then, with their permission, put the videos of them on YouTube® and on the attorneys' websites. These videos aren't professional looking; some were downright grainy. None were the typical, stand in front of your law books, tell the world how great you are videos. None offered a free consultation, but they DID offer education on aspects of DUI defense or criminal law.

Guess what? It got them clients. People saw their videos. They saw they were real people and they called them and mentioned the videos and really liked them! Would you rather spend $10,000 with a "professional video crew" to shoot self-serving, me-too junk videos for YouTube, or get this Guerrilla-style and very effective marketing done and live on the web?

For one client, we did a series of free 24-hour recorded messages on an 800 number that potential clients call. It had prerecorded information on fighting their DUI charges; and a prompt at the end of the message to 'press 1 to connect to the attorney'.

Guess what? It worked. It was a nonthreatening way to get information on their DUI case, and to call the attorney if they wished. Getting non-threatening information, without being pitched, put people at ease and got them to use the service.

So which one of these strategies I just shared makes you shake your head and assume "That would never work!", "It makes me uncomfortable", "That's unprofessional", "MY clients are different and would never respond to that kind of marketing." ??? You have to realize that these assumptions are complete BS. They're poisoning your mind. Cast them off and try this stuff.

E
XAM
INE YOUR
ASSUMPTIONS

I wouldn't write a book if such marketing didn't work. I wouldn't have testimonials if they didn't work. I wouldn't waste years of my life doing this if they didn't work. Open your litigious mind and let's move forward.☺

COUNTLESS REASONS TO TREAT POTENTIAL, CURRENT, & PAST CLIENTS LIKE GOLD (ORCHESTRATING THEIR EXPERIENCE)

Why should you make extra special effort to treat your potential clients, current clients and past clients as good as gold?

I've dealt with, talked to, and mystery shopped many a law firm. Some attorneys are amazing at converting potential clients into clients. These superhumans retain 1 in 3 people that call. Other firms are dying and couldn't retain a potential client if you stapled the client to them. These guys barely retain one in every 50 that call. There are real reasons why; and not the reasons you think.

This is a new take on an old, Golden Rule… One of the biggest factors of an attorney's success is how they and their firm (if they have partners) treat everyone they interact with.

It may be someone calling with just aclarifying question; other people are calling on their case and need serious help.There are calls from people that just retained you – they're doing a reality check to combat their buyer's remorse and make sure they made the right decision.

Other calls are from people whose case has just finished; they're in the process of becoming a past client and are at the height of their gratitude or disappointment with you; finally, old clients / past clients may be calling for new help, to refer, or with questions.

Why it is so important to treat ALL OF THESE people like gold? First of all, it doesn't cost much to do. It doesn't even take much effort, truthfully, but <u>the results can be amazing</u>.

One guy who does this successfully is my oldest client Kevin Leckerman, Esq., focusing on DUI / DWI Defense in Philadelphia and South New Jersey.

He listens to what I've told him to do the past 2 ½ years, and he actually implements a lot of advice given. He has gone through the process of looking at his entire sales process. He is treating his clients better and better. No, he's ***not kissing their asses***; just treating them really well at every stage of their interaction with him.

<u>Kevin's Case Study</u>: Kevin had 20 fewer clients in 2012, made the same money as in the previous year, and spent a ton more time with each client, allowing him to analyze their cases 100 ways to Sunday, and defend the hell out of them.

Because he had fewer clients to divide up his time amongst, and he spent a lot more time with each, clients were much happier, and <u>he had better results on more cases</u>.

Emotionally, he felt great because he had a much higher "win percentage", and he wasn't running around chasing a million clients all day.

All this in the face of RAISING his fees substantially, which allowed him the freedom to devote a ton of time to each client, and truly get them the best results possible.

So 2012 for him was great. This year is already looking great for him, as of March 2013.

Kevin and I recently talked about all the benefits we've seen come from treating everyone like gold, (and I'm about to tell you the results). When we were done, we were both amazed at our list of "benefits".

We built the list by going over why and how you should treat people well at every stage of their interaction with you and your firm.

I wrote the following from the perspective of a potential, current or past client:

Step #1: Before I've Retained You If you treat me well and give me a great experience,I am less likely to no-show appointments. This is because I am more comfortable with you, knowing you're listening to me and not coming across as an arrogant asshole.

I am less likely to tell you I have no money; I don't have enough money or you are "too expensive".

I am less likely to avoid your follow-up calls after I tell you, "I have to think it over. I'm not ready to hire you just yet."

I am less likely to have mixed feelings about hiring you and then become easy prey for cheapo bleed-them and bleed-them attorneys competing with you.

I am less likely to shut down, stop listening and not believe what you tell me; or think you only want my money and do not care about me as a person.

Step #2: **Once I have retained you & become your client** I am less likely to have buyer's remorse when I go home and tell my friends and family I hired you, only to have them say, "Why did you hire *that guy* when your Uncle Bob is a lawyer? He can help you and you shouldn't waste money on this guy."

If you treat me well and give me a great experience, I am less likely to stop making payments on a payment plan I agreed to; even though I know the judge won't let you withdraw from my case.

I am less likely to unintentionally do stupid things to hurt my ongoing case because I didn't know better; or not trust you and take matters into my own hands.

I am less likely to suffer sleepless nights and constantly worry about my case, causing me to become an emotional drain on you and your admins. I am less likely to think you are my psychologist, rather than my attorney.

Step #3: **Once you have resolved my case and I'm now a Past Client**If you thanked me for my business and keep up with me periodically even after my case is resolved, I am more likely to remember your name and refer you to my friends and family if they have legal troubles now or in the future.

I am more likely to spontaneously, or if asked; give you a good testimonial that you can put on your website to help you get more clients for years to come.

I am more likely to think back on my experience with you as a good one and always remember you as the White Knight that saved my ass. I am more likely to call you first rather than turn to Google if I have a future legal problem.

Are you impressed with this laundry list of benefits? Kevin and I sure were when we finished creating it!

It's unbelievable all the positives that happen if you craft your potential client, current client and past client experiences; if you orchestrate the big and little touches.

"Touches" can be candies, handwritten thank you notes, always being pleasant on the phone, always returning phone calls as fast as possible; as well as the big touch, which is defending each client to the absolute best of your abilities.

If You Don't Track All Your Marketing, You're Begging To Become A Marketing Victim & Get Swindled

Now let's focus on tracking and testing all your marketing. Why should you? The answer can be found in a famous quote from John Wanamaker, the first retailer to place a half-page newspaper ad in 1874. He's famous for saying, "Half of my advertising/marketing is wasted, but I don't know which half."

Wanna be a Wanamaker? Enjoy wasting thousands of dollars a month? Then stay blind when it comes to marketing and advertising spend. Better to assume, hope, think, project and imagine it's working.

Even worse, many draw erroneous conclusions without the facts (remember, you guys are attorneys and this is your language). "Google Pay per ClickDoesn't Work", "Direct Mail makes money but I think it's a breakeven", "SEO is hit and miss". Oh yeah? How MUCH does A make you vs. B vs C? How much does it cost you to get a warm body to sign your retainer agreement? How much too even get someone in the door for a "free consultation" you're paying $800 in marketing for?

In my experience talking with hundreds of attorneys, 95%+ don't track their marketing…at all.

This is a serious problem.

Before we get into any kind of marketing, whether social media, pay-per-click, newsletters, whatever, remember, there's barely any point to it unless you track the results.

If you don't or won't track your marketing, ***I guarantee you are or will be a victim of advertising vampires and marketing vultures and you will deserve what little results you get.***

Once you track a particular type of marketing, you get the secondary benefit of testing, tweaking, and optimizing that channel to make it EVEN MORE PROFITABLE.

A "marketing channel" may be Yellow Pages, Google pay-per-click, your website, business card, newsletter, newspaper ad, etc.Each one is a marketing channel. Track each separately, to root out the winners and losers, the money makers vs. the bloodsuckers.

Nowadays, there's really no excuse not to do it, given that phone and email tracking is so cheap and so sophisticated.

You can track phone calls. You can track people who complete a form on your website. You can track walk-ins. You can track anything under the sun for a few bucks a month in an automated way.

Don't tell me you actually ENJOY getting hounded by calls every single day from marketing vultures saying, "We'll get you on the 1st page of Google. We'll do this. We'll do that. We'll put you in the Yellow Pages. We'll put you in our directory. You'll get a flood of clients."

You know most of these are empty, bullshit promises.

Still, a lot of attorneys fall prey to the vampires and vultures. They spend 3, 5, even $10,000 a month, and they have no clue what's really going on with their marketing.

Yes, I know you've been burned by marketers before. Most attorneys have, and it's their own damn fault.

Either you or a colleague (I guarantee) has spent thousands a month, only to realize the phone's not ringing.

Don't want to be burned again? Replace Fear with Facts... TRACK!

Let's beat this point to death, because it's vital you understand not only 'why should', but 'what's the benefit'.
My attorney clients, whether I bug them or they do it themselves, can sleep well at night because they know they're not wasting money.

If a marketing channel isn't making money, they know QUICKLY, and can either tweak it to profitability, or get rid of it if it won't respond.

Another benefit? My attorney clients know, as their marketing consultant, if I am not doing my job; I cannot bullshit my way out of it. These guys are tracking the results, because I made them do it, and I'm accountable and so are they for converting the leads coming from their marketing into retained clients.

Wouldn't you like to know if that guy overseeing pay-per-click for you is doing anything, or just taking your money every month? You work hard for your money. You have to see where it is going and what it is doing.

What Does It Mean to Be Profitable? What Is ROI and Why Is It a True Measure of Results?

Thankfully, you'll find some marketing channels to be truly profitable, meaning they return 2, 3, 4 or 5x your money (which is called return on investment, or ROI).

For example, let's say direct mail is returning 3x your money, but pay-per-click is losing you 50% of the money you put in. Yellow Pages is a breakeven dollar-wise, but an actual loser because of time

spent going to and sitting in court and filing paperwork, as well as your office overhead, pulls it down from a breakeven to a 35% loss.

Direct mail is a 300% ROI, PPC is -50% ROI, and Yellow Pages is -35% ROI in this example.

Now imagine a broken change machine at a casino. You put in $20 and get back $100 change. Huh? You try the machine again with another $20 and it spits out $100 again.

How long and how fast are you going to feed this machine with twenties? As fast and as quietly as you can, because you're getting a 5:1 ROI on your money.

And that is the power of a successful marketing channel that is tracked and is earning you a positive ROI – it's like a money machine you should want to feed as much as possible.

What do most attorneys do instead? They cry and say, "PayPer Click is expensive, I hate it" or "Each direct mail letter I send out costs me $2.75 – that's expensive". Both are meaningless statements; the ROI you get from a marketing channel is what REALLY matters.

Watch Out! Losers Can Drag Down Winners

Let's say you spend $5,000 a month on marketing, in three different channels. Two of them are returning $8,000 a month, and the third is losing you $3,000 a month.

You spent $5,000 and took in $8,000 + $8,000 - $3,000 = $13,000. That's a 2.66x ROI right? (We're ignoring time in court and paperwork and admin salaries, i.e. "overhead")

This isn't a bad scenario – what's the problem here? Well, if you didn't track your marketing, this would be invisible to you, and you'd merrily go along, netting $13k - $5k = $8k a month, probably frustrated you're not making more.

If you tracked and found there was a loser in the bunch, you could cut the loser if it couldn't be rehabbed and improved.

Now watch the magic of getting rid of the albatross around your neck and cutting out the loser:

You were spending $1,000 a month on the loser, so your monthly spend has decreased to $4,000.

Your gross is now $8k + $8k = $16k and your net is now $16k - $4k = **$12k**vs $8k, **a $4,000 BONUS PER MONTH**.

You'd have to take on 2 additional cases a month to make this extra $4,000. Over a year, this would be 2 * 12 = 24 additional clients, wasting hundreds of hours of your time.
You'd profit an ADDITIONAL $4k * 12 = **$48,000 a year.**

Yes, it IS possible to have ridiculously profitable results just from tracking, testing and tweaking your marketing.

Tracking frees you up to cut out true losers without any compunction or fear.

Let's take this even further to see what's possible…

How about doubling down on winners in addition to cutting out losers?

Maybe you are doing direct mail, and you were afraid to expand it. Once tracked, you see that it's really pulling in a 300% ROI. Double down on that spend, (i.e. send your letters twice or include a 3D lumpy mail item - more about this later) and ride that winner home.

It's possible to grow that one channel from 300% to 400 or 500% ROI, net of increased spend, which would be minimal.

What Should Be Tracked? Phone Calls? Emails? What Does 'Cost to Aquire a Customer' Mean?

What should you track? A result for you is a phone call, email, text or web form filled out from a person who has a legal issue in your practice areas. Typically phone is the top way most attorneys get leads. People may also fill in a web form on your website or send an email or text, but leads don't come nearly as frequently that way. All ways must be tracked, however.

Tracking can teach you a very important concept called **Cost to Acquire a Customer**.

Let's say you spend $1 for each person that clicks an ad to get to your website. Tracking shows you that 1 of every 200 clickers pick up the phone and call you. (By the way, these are not unrealistic numbers - conversion online is very low)

This means you spent $200 to ***just get a lead to call you***, nevermind RETAIN YOU! ($1/click * 200 clicks/call)

It gets even more expensive. It gets even scarier...

How many potential clients that call do you actually RETAIN? (call to conversion ratio) Let's say you retain 1:3

($200/call * 3 calls/retention) = **$600** to get a warm body in your chair, signing a retainer.

Now consider what you charge on a run of the mill, no trial, simple case. If you charge $1,000 and it costs you $600 to get a case, that's not much of a profit margin. With court time and overhead, **you may actually lose money working on a case like this!**

What if a basic case is worth $2,500 to you on average (because you treat everyone like gold and don't offer the lowest price) and you're spending only $600?

Well, now you have 450% ROI, and you're making good money from your advertising. See why you gotta know your numbers?
It's a very worthwhile endeavor to figure out how much it costs you to get a client from each marketing channel. I promise you'll be very surprised how much it costs nowadays.

For most attorneys I deal with, it costs $500 to $1,000 to get and retain each client, sometimes a lot more.

Moral of the Story: If your prices are way low, you may be starving to death and not know exactly why. Know your cost to retain a client, get a phone call, email, text or webform filled in, and know each lead is damn expensive and precious and must not be wasted with bad follow up.

Marketing & Advertising Is The Front End Of Your Sales Funnel… "Mommy, What's a Sales Funnel?"

A sales funnel is the series of steps a stranger takes on the path to becoming your retained client, from encountering your marketing, ad, or advertising, all the way through signing your retainer agreement, through representation, through to past client status and beyond.

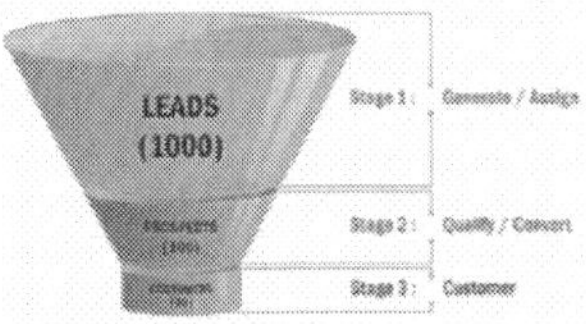

Once a potential client calls, emails, texts, or fills in a webform, a typical attorney will have a two or three-step sales funnel before retention occurs. We'll focus on this part.

Let's say a potential client calls and you talk to them. They either make an appointment for an initial consult, or say, "I'm going to ask around and call you back." That is the 1st step of this part of your sales funnel.

A lot of attorneys lose people at Stage 1 for various reasons like mishandling calls and interactions, but also in large part because they never follow up. They lose 80%+ of the people who call because the prospect is unqualified, they're just a tire kicker or freeloader, or the attorney bungled the interaction, didn't inspire trust, build rapport, and caused the person to price shop or get a 2nd opinion.

Yes, I know there are many price shoppers, tire kickers, and mentally ill people who have no intention of retaining EVER.

I can only help you with the ones who have at least some merit, so let's focus on those…

Moving along your sales funnel, we get to **appointment setting stage**. Some firms have tons of no-shows, some convert most callers on the phone, without even needing an in-office appointment!

If you have got lots of no-shows or even a consistent percentage, one big reason is you're not following up with potential clients and reducing their "buyer's remorse" before their appointment time, which may be 2, 3 or 5 days in the future.

(We'll go much deeper into follow-up in the attorney-author-authority-process "speak a book" section of this book)

Remember, your appointments are being lured away by the siren's song of other attorneys, and the negative comments from friends, family, and a spouse or parent.

As a potential client moves further along your funnel, the money you've spent to get those increases, and so each stage becomes more important to manage and patch holes.

Imagine the person going down this funnel, getting closer and closer to the end point where they are signing your retainer agreement and putting money in your pocket.

Moving along the funnel to **Step 3** where the potential successfully makes it in for an appointment. They're in your office; you have spent $500 - $1,000 or more, plus a lot of time and effort just to get them in the door.

Are you going to convert them to a retained client, or are they going to say, "Well, I've got to talk to my wife. I'll be back?"

Will you hear: "You're too expensive;" or "I don't have the money;" or "I don't have enough money?"

We will talk about strategies to help you minimize all of these problems, but realize this is another step in your funnel, and a lot is at stake at this point!

Diagnose Your Sales Funnel – Where's The Biggest Leak?

When you look at your sales funnel, you'll see you're losing most of your clients at a certain step, versus the other ones. You want to fix this hole in your hose, because it's where the most water (MONEY) is leaking out. Only by knowing what your funnel is and tracking and examining each step will you know where you are losing people. You'll surprise yourself when you identify the problem and think, "Oh my God, we're losing a lot of people here. I didn't know."

Rich, I Should Track All My Marketing, But My Sales Funnel Isn't The Problem...Once People Contact My Office, We Retain Most Of Them... BULLSHIT!

Ever Mystery Shop your own practice? You'd probably cringe and want to crawl inside your own skin and hide if you did.

Using a disclaimer, of course, you want to record every incoming call, and every person who answers the phone, including **you**, your admins and any attorneys working with or for you.

Not necessarily you say? I hear people screwing up potential client interactions and LOSING CUSTOMERS at over 90% of law firms I've Mystery Shopped.

Secretaries blurt out, "*Law Office*." They mishandle callers and make them nervous. They don't build rapport by asking a caller about their situation gently.

They drive potential clients away.

How'd you like to hear callers to your firm sit on hold for 5 minutes before hanging up? How about 50% of callers told "the attorney's not in, do you want their voicemail?"

A recent article on Car Dealerships said **20% of all calls go unanswered.** Think about that next time someone cries that "we're in a bad economy… waaaah!"

I've heard countless secretaries / admins talk rudely to people and who then hang up on them. Many attorneys are, frankly, and for lack of a better word, ASSHOLES to callers.

Are you an asshole? Are you a terse, unhelpful, "I can't tell you anything, you have to come into my office" attorney?

You'd be shocked (or perhaps not) how many law firms are complete jerks to potential callers.

This lack of attention can cost you dozens of lost clients, and $50,000 a year or more… EASILY.

I know you don't want to do it, but here's a hugely ignored area of marketing / advertising that is rarely tracked, tested, and tweaked.

Who wants to step on the scale when you're 400 pounds? Who wants to hear from the doctor they've got diabetes and high blood pressure? No one - that's why you must track NOW so you don't mysteriously die of a financial disease later and never be the wiser.

Make sure you look at all your personnel. Each one represents their own ROI - are they are contributing or taking away from the firm?

Analyzing all your personnel and their individual ROI / performance will help you diagnose if you've got a hidden nasty critter in your office that's sabotaging your conversion.

Let's say you have 2 other attorneys working for you and a couple of admins. You want to track how many potential clients each one is interacting with vs. how many are retained - you may find one that has a much lower (or higher) fallout rate and that will help identify the problem.

Then you can "re-educate" or fire that person and learn from the top performer. (Give the top performer a raise, too - incentivize all staff including yourself)

Easiest, Cheapeast & Most Effective Tracking Methods Around

So how do you track? Thankfully, it's easy and cheap nowadays. For phone tracking, you can use services like If by Phone (ifbyphone.com), which I highly recommend.

Ifbyphone is about $72 a month for a master account and each phone number you get- whether local or a 1800 number, costs about $3 per month per number. It is ridiculously cheap, and you can have each call recorded, forwarded, and tracked if you wish.

Put unique phone numbers that forward to your main phone# on every marketing channel you use; each will then be tracked - it's simple, effective as well as eye-opening.

Where can you put tracking phone numbers? On billboards, on your business card, your website, everywhere. For clients, I put tracking numbers on direct mail letters, billboards, Yellow Pages ads, pay per click, business cards, on different office locations.

As many places as makes sense and where tracking is needed.

A common frustration I hear is, "We have clients call us, but we don't know where they come from. When asked how they were referred to us, people say the internet or they don't know." Well this way, you will know. You don't have to depend on people's bad memories.

You will know this person called from our billboard because that's the only place you used that unique phone#. This person called off direct mail; that one called from a newsletter… and this guy? He called from our website, not just "the internet" or "google".
Phone tracking is a VERY powerful tool; and very easy. What makes it even better is the data it gives you, such as:

The date and time someone calls, their caller ID, the # of minutes they were connected, what marketing channel they came in on, and if you wish, literally what was said if you're using call recording.

This is a real fast way to get a pulse on a new marketing idea or evaluate an existing marketing method. You'll quickly know if that newspaper ad, pay per click campaign, or online lead service is bringing in calls.

Also, tracking web form submissions and emails is very easy to set up on your website. If someone fills in and submits a form, it's a no brainer to track and can be set up in minutes.

Once Tracking Is Set Up, The Best, Centralized Reporting Tool Is SmartSheet.com

Getting tracking data is great, but if it's a pain in the ass to assemble it, if it can't be updated in real time, if multiple people in your firm need to update the results on the fly, then you need SmartSheet.com

(**Disclaimer:** SmartSheet and IfByPhone do not compensate me for recommending them - I love both services, however)

Everyone in your firm has to be committed to putting all the results for a given day in a common place like Smart Sheet, a shared online Excel sheet.

You can have it set up so every phone call and every email that comes in goes into one sheet that everyone can share and see it at all times. So when a phone call comes in, Jane upfront can update that it was a solicitor. When another phone call comes in, Joe the attorney can say, "Oh, I talked to them and we have an appointment for next Tuesday."

Over a week or a month you'll have a simple report that says, "This month we got 34 phone calls, and 5 webforms filled in. Of all leads, 9 were potential clients and we retained 6 of them. Their names were X, Y, and Z, and 4 of them came from our website. 1 of them came from direct mail. 1 of them came from a newsletter."

"Attorney Mike retained 3 of them. Jane, the admin, was involved in 4 of the 6 retainees. It cost us $642 per client for the 4 website retentions, $783 for the direct mail client, and $376 for the newsletter client. Total gross revenue from all 6 clients was $17,400."

See the power of knowing all of this through tracking and finding out exactly what is happening in your firm? Look at the difference between knowing this level of detail vs. hoping, guessing, and praying.

Final note: In order for this to work you have to make it **mandatory** that all your personnel, including you as the attorney, update this shared spreadsheet at least 3x a day; or whenever a client calls, emails or comes in.

Get tracking and grow your practice. There's no excuse.

Hollywood Uses Scripts... and So Must You, Your Partner Attorneys, and All Staff Members

Everyone in your firm that interacts with potential, current, and past clients should use scripts. I'm not talking about just your admins, your secretaries, your answering service and other attorneys in the firm. I am talking about **YOU**, too...

Why? There are 3 very important reasons.

#1 - You want to give potentials, current clients and past clients a continuously positive and fantastic experience when they call your law firm. (yes, it IS possible to have a good experience calling a law firm) In the "treating clients like Gold" section, you can read about the myriad reasons that a great experience is vital to a successful practice.

#2 – Are you being sabotaged by rude, apathetic admins, secretaries, answering services or other attorneys in your firm? You may be sabotaging yourself by answering the phone rudely, not building rapport, and not scripting your calls as well. (many attorneys are in for a nasty surprise when their practice is mystery shopped, only to find that THEY are the biggest problem)

#3 - Wouldn't you love to cut out the daily, relentless, phone calls from solicitors draining your and your staff's time?

There's a lot of time wasters out there – solicitors, court personnel, tire kickers and people with no money. A lot of attorneys blow 1 – 2 hours a day on the phone with these knuckleheads.

Think about it. How many times a day does your office phone or cellphone ring? If you're answering most or all the calls, then you are getting way too many annoying calls from marketing companies, tire kickers and time wasters; and too few from potential clients.

You have to use your time wisely.

What if you have your personnel trained to screen effectively, only letting qualified prospect calls through? What if you cut out all the garbage?

I bet you would save at least an hour a day, and to an attorney, that's huge. So sharpen your gatekeepers' teeth. Train them to stick and move like Muhammad Ali did and filter, screen, and block bad calls, while letting good ones through.

Here's a powerful sample script that filters like a charm:

Instead of answering the phone with, "Law office", your admins should instead say "Law Office of XYZ. This is Mary. Are you calling with a legal problem we can help you with?"

Why say this?

Right off the bat, the caller has to identify themselves as good vs. garbage; a welcome guest vs. an annoying pest; a potential client vs. a waste of time. If a caller does NOT have a legal problem, this question will help filter them out.

Let's say the caller gets sneaky and says, "I'd like to speak to Attorney XYZ." What should your gatekeeper say in this instance?

"Attorney XYZ devotes his time to working on current client issues and talking to new potential clients who want his undivided attention and help."

"Do you need legal help, or are you a current client?"

Train them to sit and wait for the answer. The caller must then respond and say if they are a current client or that they truly want legal help.

A caller may then say: "Well, I'm calling to speak to him about a marketing plan" or "I'm just trying to find out how much he charges."

If they don't need legal help and they're not a current client, the gatekeeper should say, "Please give me a brief description of what you are going to tell Attorney XYZ before I see if he's available. I do not want to upset him by interrupting his important client work without good reason."

Once again, you're forcing people to qualify and filter themselves. You're not being mean, however a caller must have a deserving reason to get through to the busy attorney who wants to focus on his/her clients. What's mean about that?

See how this script acts as a powerful filter?

Most folks who aren't potential clients won't get through to waste your time and your day. Court personnel can be handled by the admin. Marketers can be screened out, forced to send an email, or blocked completely.

Furthermore, you can CHOOSE to take certain calls from certain types of people when it's convenient for YOU. No more fighting fires all day; if you're truly in need of new marketing, for instance, you can block off a 2 hour chunk on a Thursday morning to handle marketing calls, for example.

- This script will save you at least an hour+ a day.
- It will improve your ability to retain new clients and improve your relationship with existing clients.
- Current clients will know you are focused on their cases and that you take their situations very seriously… because your admin said so!
- Potential clients will know you focus heavily on your current clients and they will get that same dedication once they retain you.
- Solicitors, court personnel and other potential time wasters filter themselves out. They'll feel bad for disturbing you because you appealed to their better nature, saying, "This guy is working on important stuff. If you're not calling about that, I don't want to bother him."

Although scripts can be lifesavers and game changers, I guarantee most attorneys reading this will find an excuse NOT to do it.

Here are the most common Assumptions / Excuses:
"Oh, my secretary won't do this. She's been with me for 6 years. I can't tell her to do this now."

"We don't have a problem with how we answer the phone. We're fine. Answering the phone, "Law office" works just fine for us."

"I really don't get that many calls. This isn't going to help."

"I don't want to push away potential clients, and screening them would push them away."

"Clients know I'm a lawyer. I'm busy and they shouldn't waste my time anyway, so I don't need this." I've heard these excuses and assumptions a million times.

Don't fear scripting – welcome it. Why get in your own way and stop yourself from succeeding, like stepping on the gas pedal while the car's in park?

Shave 5 hours a week off your work schedule. Spend more time with your spouse and kids. Give yourself time to think, plan, and run a business. **Stop fighting fires all day and put scripting to work for you.**

How Answering Your Phones The Wrong Way Will Cost You Thousands

Now that you're convinced you should script your calls, I 'm going to give examples of bad vs. good scripting.

When a potential calls your law office and you blurt out: "LAW OFFICE." It makes callers immediately uncomfortable and many will stutter and get nervous. **Bad way to start**.

You didn't say which law office they called. You didn't greet them. You didn't say your name.

Seeking some sign of human life, a caller may uncomfortably say: "I..is… is thi..this the law office of John Smith?" Identify yourself with a warmer greeting such as, "Law office of Jones, Jones and Smith. This is Sarah. Do you have a legal issue we can help you with?"

Now they know **where they called**, who they're talking to, and a question has been put to them that they must answer.

Sounds obvious, right? Common sense is not very common.

Let's continue with the bad script. Someone says, "Law office" and the caller stammers, "Hi, I uh, got arrested last night for drunk driving. Are you an attorney? Can you help me?"

The admin says, "No, Mr. Smith is the attorney. He's on the phone right now. Can I take a message?" The caller says, "Never mind, I'll call back. Bye."

This EXACT SCENARIO is so common, it's scary.

Well, now you lost a potential. Why? You made them uncomfortable. They didn't know if you were an attorney or an admin when they called. They had to tell you their problem, like calling out in the darkness, "Is anybody there?" If the caller DOESN'T hang up, you're still off on a very bad foot.

Many law offices are very unfriendly. Believe me, it's very intimidating to call an attorney.

You probably have no concept of what it's like to be facing criminal charges. You've never been a defendant. Sure, you've spoken to many, but being one yourself is a completely different animal.

People are emotional, upset, frightened, and freaked out.

They've been questioned by police, handcuffed, arrested, embarrassed, and sat in jail overnight or longer.

If a potential client's calling you, and you or your admins are assholes, they're going to hang up or at least question you, your motives, your experience, your fees, everything.

Here's another bad script: "LAW OFFICE.", the phone is answered. "Hi, uh do you guys know if a 2nd shoplifting charge in six years counts as a first time or not?"

The admin says, "You'll have to ask Attorney Smith. Let me transfer you to him." You didn't answer the person's question. Meanwhile, some firms put callers on hold for 5+ minutes, and the caller hangs up. By just transferring the caller and not telling them your name or asking simple screening questions, you've already dropped the ball.

The admin could have said, "Mr. Smith has worked with many clients who have similar situations. He'll be able to give you the details you need to handle this. I'm very sorry this happened to you. Please hold for a minute. I'm going to transfer you right away."

How much better does that sound versus, "Duh, I don't know anything? Let me transfer you."

When the call is transferred, how do you, as the attorney, answer? "This is Attorney Smith." is NOT a good greeting.

There's no intro from your admin - it's not a warm transfer. The caller has to start again with their question: "Hi. Does it count if you have 2 shoplifting charges in six years as a first offense?"

Making the caller repeat their question further intimidates them. They're starting to become annoyed, irritated and obviously stressed out. They're already on guard and suspicious.

Furthermore, they <u>haven't been given any indication</u> your law office "fights for you," "is aggressive," "has 10,000 years' experience," "is board-certified;" or any of that meaningless crap attorneys put on their marketing. You haven't done a single thing to show benefit or differentiate yourself, even before you start interacting with a potential client.

Here's a much better way to handle the call: The admin says, "Mr. Smith has worked with many clients who have similar situations. He'll be able to give you the details you need to handle this. I'm very sorry this happened to you. Please hold for a minute. I'm going to transfer you right away." (same as before)

THEN, she calls the attorney and says "Hi, Attorney Smith. This is Sarah up front. I've got Bob on the phone. He's dealing with a 2nd shoplifting charge in six years. He had a question for you as to whether that counts as a first offense or second. Can I put him through?"

Sarah then returns to the caller and gets the attorney on the line with the caller and says: "Bob, this is Attorney Smith. He will definitely be able to help you with your shoplifting question." The attorney then says, "Hi Bob. I appreciate you calling. Sarah, we'll take it from here - thank you."

Sarah says, in closing, "Thanks for calling Bob. I'll let you two talk things over. I'm hanging up now."

You tell me: **How much better is that script** versus a cold transfer with no hand-off?

See why scripting can radically improve your retention rates and earn you more money without even spending money on additional marketing?

Let's talk about what happens vs. what you should do during an initial phone consult with a potential client...

You're on the phone with a potential, and they've described their situation briefly. Typical attorneys say, "Well, the law says this and that, and the maximum penalties are X, Y and Z. You really have to come in for an appointment, and then we can go into your situation in depth. I can't say much or promise anything on the phone. You gotta come in."

Instead of spending quality time on the phone... 10 minutes, 20 minutes, even 30 minutes talking to a prospect and building rapport, most attorneys want to get them in the office to close them. They're afraid to spend time on the phone for fear of wasting time and/or losing the potential client.

Sadly, just 'trying to get 'em in the office' often backfires and lowers your retention percentage... Why?

Even though your answers, using the above script are factual, they're **unemotional.**

- You're not addressing the true need of the person calling.
- You're not providing information.

- You're not building trust and rapport.
- **You're not giving any reason why and how you are different from any other attorney they might talk to.**

How's a prospect supposed to figure out if they should come see you vs. calling other attorneys if you haven't done any of the above bullet points?

Want to know what most callers will say or think, based on just trying to get them in the office?

"It's okay, thanks. 'Click.'", or
"I have to talk to my wife, and then call you back. Bye."

Once they hang up, they're NEVER going to call you back and **you know it**.

Off they go, looking for another attorney that's not rude to them, offers zero information, and tries to just "get them into the office."

Hopefully this doesn't sound too familiar, if you're even lucky enough to get this far, because your admin, secretary, or answering service didn't screw it up even before the call got to you!

What's a better way to handle calls from potential clients?

The attorneys I work with that sometimes retain up to 30% of ALL LEADS, spend ~30 minutes on the phone with each potential client. They explain every step of the case process, give the likely sequence of events, explain the law and possible defenses, all the while evaluating and qualifying the potential client to see if it's worthwile investing time in defending them.

By the end of a properly executed call, guess what happens?

➔ A lot of these attorneys **retain over the phone**.

They don't even need the caller to come to the office. They have much fewer no-shows, delays, or chance for other attorneys to swoop in and seduce them away.

This is because **they did all the work of building rapport, educating, trust-building and screening on the phone.**

Instead of believing you're WASTING TIME, there is no better time spent building rapport, hearing their fact pattern, educating them, demonstrating you're a human being, an attorney who cares, is personable, and has special skills that will be of good use to them.

If you don't do this, how's a prospect ever going to know that you're different, special, board-certified, caring, aggressive, or any of that brandinggobbledygook that most attorneys put out?

Remember, Hollywood scripts, and so must you.

SMASH YOUR COMPETITION BY AUTHORING A BOOK. GET THE CREDIBILITY, AUTHORITY & CELEBRITY YOU NEED TO DOMINATE

- ➔ Authoring a book is not NEARLY as hard or time-sucking as you think, so don't get worried.

Authoring a book by 'speaking it', is a unique method I developed called the "Attorney-Author-Authority-Process."

First of all, why go through the trouble?

Let's say your doctor tells you you're barely three months away from a deadly heart attack and you have to call the heart specialist ASAP.
Can you simply call your favorite heart surgeon on their cell phone and book an appointment that's convenient for you?

The top specialists are booked for months, and you know it. **If you are lucky**, you'll get an appointment 2 weeks out, on a day and time not of your choosing, but probably the last open slot the doc has.

When this doctor sees you, you're going to tell him, "Thank you so much for seeing me Doc."

You're THANKING someone who you're going to pay $100,000 for seeing you? Think about that.

Yes, it makes perfect sense to do so; you don't question that it's going to be hard to even get in to see the doctor. Hell no, you're not going to get their cell phone number. You don't even ask.

Once the heart specialist looks you over and prescribes a treatment regimen (which will include life-threatening, but necessary surgery) are you going to argue? No way.

Whatever he tells you to do, you will listen... Why?

The heart surgeon has AUTHORITY. CREDIBILITY. CELEBRITY. EXCLUSIVITY.

Why can't <u>you</u> have this as an attorney? Can you? YES.

Although it won't magically transform you into the #1 guy in criminal defense in your area, authoring a book will give you Authority, Credibility and Celebrity. It will improve your positioning with potential clients, big time, if you use it properly, as I'm going to describe shortly.

Let's talk in terms you'll intimately know:

Who would you hire to defend your DUI, fight for custody of your kids in a nasty divorce, defend your drug possession case, handle your $2.5 million dollar estate, ensure you get disability payments, fight to settle your workman's comp claim or to get you compensation for a car accident?

Choices A, B, C, D, etc are your typical attorneys who say, "I'm aggressive; I'll fight for you; I have 30 years of experience. I'm board certified. I'm a former prosecutor."

The Authority Choice is the attorney who can not only say the above, but also say: Please take this copy of my book on this particular subject called '10 Ways to Defend Your XYZ Case.' Even if we're not a fit to work together, you'll get a LOT of useful information from reading it."

Not everyone, but the majority will be swayed, impressed, and more likely to hire the guy who wrote the book.

In my mind, the attorney who authored a book instantly grows 4 inches taller, looks more handsome, seems nicer, becomes more authoritative, knowledgeable, and "expert-like", turning into the Suze Orman of DUI, the Doctor Phil of Estate Planning, the F. Lee Bailey or Johnny Cochran of criminal defense. **Who would YOU rather hire?**

<u>**Some amazing stats to consider:**</u>

- ➔ Attorney authors have up to a 1/3 LOWER no-show rate when their book is overnighted thru Fed Ex to a potential client before their scheduled appointment, in a package that includes testimonials, a personal letter, and the attorney's book.

- ➔ Reduces excuses clients give you when they don't hire you: "I'll be back" "Let me talk to my wife;" "Let me get back to you" "You're too expensive;" or "I don't have any money."

If you've been procrastinating writing a book for 7 years because you hate writing or just don't have the time, **I can interview a spoken book out of you in 1 HOUR FLAT.**

Yes, the process takes 1hr of your time and about an hour more for corrections… who can complain about 2 freaking hours of work to WRITE A BOOK?

A minimal amount of work and time gets you a book that will earn you **AT LEAST 1 additional client a month for 2 years into the future**, or longer unless the law changes dramatically in your practice areas.

If your clients are worth $2,500 each to you, that's:
$2,500/client * 1/month * 12mo/yr = **$60,000 a YEAR.**
Finally, it's EASY to write 1, 2, 3 or more books, each on a separate area of your practice or sub-area.
(ex: 1st time DUI, Car Accidents, etc)

It is a heck of a lot easier than it sounds, isn't it? Don't be afraid; be EXCITED about what it will do for your business, your Credibility, your Authority and your Celebrity as an attorney.

You will dramatically increase your income, retention ratio and the quality of clients you get; a **no brainer for sure.**

THE BACKSTORY OF HOW THE ATTORNEY AUTHOR AUTHORITY PROCESS CAME TO PASS...

For 3 years, I started in the legal industry byproviding 34,982+ DUI leads to attorneys nationwide through group legal advertising on myDUIattorney.org.

I went into this business with a bit of fear and loathing about dealing with lawyers. Attorneys can be mean and standoffish when you first meet them, and even when you get to know them, but I quickly grew to like the hard working, ethics-driven guys and gals out there who save many an ass-in-a-sling.

My 1st strategy to improve an attorney's Celebrity, Authority and Credibility in the surrounding areas they serve was to conduct a free video interview thru Skype® to be posted on YouTube and linked to their website.

Attorney'sfeedback included: "Potentials saw my video on the web and they really liked it." These potentials ended up hiring them and mentioned liking their videos as a deciding factor; fantastic - a step forward already!

These videos were helping attorneys get clients, and the ones I interviewed would beat out other local guys because the interviews provided personal exposure to the attorney potentials were seeking. Potentials' seeing what the attorney looks like, hearing how they sound helped them grasp how that particular lawyer thinks, acts, and would interact with them if hired... all this from the safety of the internet.

Comments from potential clients were: "I felt I got to know you before I even met you" or"Your videos made me feel comfortable." That led to lawyers being hired more often.

These video interviews, surprisingly, even started showing up on the blessed 1st page of Google - the Holy Grail for most attorneys, getting more exposure.

After I did about 30 of these interviews and talked to dozens more lawyers, I learned the ins, outs and industry insider realty of being an attorney: overworked, underpaid, the whole world on a payment plan; clients that stop paying; misguided judges not letting you withdraw.

I learned about 80-hour work weeks, battling lowball, newbie attorney competition; price-shopping potentials; no-shows and deal-killing secretaries.

In my travels, and mainly at marketing seminars, I began running into super lawyers. I don't mean the magazine "Super Lawyers," but super successful lawyers who all happened to attribute this to good marketing.

One DUI and reckless speeding attorney I met makes $500,000+ a year and gets well over 20 phone leads a day – he handed me his iPhone and let me scroll down through the leads that day in his email!

Another savant in California who does Estate Planning has a 96% closing rate, once potentials come to his office for a consult – simply amazing.

A car accident personal injury guy in Canada that uses a newsletter to past clients to earn him **77% of all his new client business from past client referrals**.

Amazing attorneys, doing amazing things.

It didn't take more than a few conversations to see the commonality amongst these super successful lawyers... They all said providing useful information & education to potentials through a book they had authored was a major leg their success stood on. Their books, they insisted, established them as an Authority; not a cheapo, bleed 'em and plead 'em attorney. They became minor celebrities in their niche and local area and whooped the competition's collective asses.

Potential clients, they insisted, were **attracted** to the non-threatening, educational resources they put out. Potential clients started calling more often while the tire kicking and the price shopping died way down; clients were coming to them vs. them having to hunt and kill on a daily basis.

Motivated by what I heard, I adopted their book-mongering process, and developed the

Attorney Author Authority Process
(how it works)

You and I schedule a 15 minute discovery call to see if the Attorney-Author-Authority Process is right for you. You choose how many books you're going to "speak" and their specific topics (ex: DUI, juvenile law, car accidents, drug cases, sex crimes, divorce, estate planning).

No one's ever caught off guard by the questions, because they're all disclosed beforehand. Even if I have no experience with a topic, I ask you the most common questions potential clients ask you, on a daily basis, as well as the layman's "urban myth" type questions you're likely to be asked, based on my television and mass media "education".

The goal is to re-create you in print. Your style, mannerisms, knowledge, and experience, on paper. A facsimile of your best phone consultation; your most compelling statements that turn prospects into retained clients. A non-threatening, "best of you" guide book.

Then we schedule a 60 min, recorded, Q&A, interview-style phone call. The whole call gets transcribed, and the ums, yeahs, uhs and other false starts get edited out of the transcription.

My team then creates a title and cover design, puts in testimonials, lays out the interior, makes chapters, adds relevant pictures and contact information and sets up the whole book. Disclaimers that the book is purely informational and not to be taken as legal advice are added. Creation of an attorney-client relationship is also disclaimed.

You then review the final cleaned-up product and make final edits. **Within 3 weeks you have a ready-to-print, ready to publish BOOK that you've authored**.

Now watch all the places your book can go; where it can be used, re-used, re-purposed, and made to help you:

Place #1 - the book becomes downloadable PDF-format e-book. We modify your website's design so people can see a picture of the book cover, called an e-cover. It looks like a real book on the web, and there is a download button for a free download.

When a potential client clicks to download your free book, they're asked to enter their name, phone number and email. The pdf then downloads to their computer, and their information is captured and emailed to you. They've now "raised their hand" and become a lead you can call on and email. By downloading your free book, they've expressed interest in the topic, and silently said, "Mr. Attorney, I've downloaded your book because I'm interested in the subject and have a legal issue; Please contact me."

I highly encourage you to contact them later that day or the next day. Ask how they found your book, what prompted them to download it, and start building rapport.

Place #2 – A one hour call typically turns into approximately 7,000 transcribed words, which then gets chopped up into a series of 11-14 articles that are placed appropriately, by subject, on your website. This dramatically increases your website's content and makes you more likely to get Google, Yahoo and Bing organic searches. Your website becomes a compelling resource for searchers. It helps you SEO-wise and website-wise for years to come.

Some of my attorney clients have smartly invested 8-10 hours of their time to create multiple books, and add 60,000 – 80,000 additional words (100+ articles) to their websites.

…these same attorneys have seen their organic traffic quadruple or more and their phones start ringing as well.

Place #3 - The books are physically printed. Many attorneys cringe at this step and how to effectively use the physical version of their book… **But the #1, Most Critical, Most Useful Way to use your book is to print physical copies and mail / hand them out to potential clients. (more on this shortly)**

First of all, printing is NOT expensive. An initial order of 100 copies comes to you within 7 business days of order. The cost is $350-400, including shipping ($3.50 - $4.00 each)

You'll feel a sense of pride and accomplishment the day you receive your box o' books, tear it open, and hold them in your hands.

Place #4 - Take pictures of yourself proudly holding and displaying your book. Why? Again, it establishes your Credibility, Authority and Celebrity. Guess where you put these pictures?

They go on your website, on a Yellow Pages ad; on your business card, billboard, bus stop, on your office walls, everywhere. Any piece of marketing you have can use this picture to amplify your credibility. Let's say you do direct mail. Instead of standing in front of a shelf of law books, include a picture of you standing there holding a book you wrote. It makes a big difference.

The Most Effective and Important Way To Utilize Your Physical Book?

As previously mentioned, you have what is called a sales funnel. Potential clients contact you by phone or email, and go through a series of steps and either become a retained client or not.

Here's how to use your book to plug the holes in your sales funnel that are costing you $10,000 a month, possibly more:

Scenario #1: A Potential calls you and you engage in a phone consult. It sounds like they've got a solid fact pattern, and they'd make a good, profitable client, but they don't make an appointment. Instead, they spend 15-30 minutes with you or your admin on the phone and then say, "I'm going to call some other attorneys and get back to you;" or "I'm going to talk to my wife about it;" or "Let me think about it." ***Shit. I've wasted my time and they aren't coming back. What do I do?***

Typically, the transition from potential to ghost starts... You call them a couple of times, send an email or two, but they disappear into thin air and never return your advances again. What should you do instead?

Train your admin and yourself so anytime a potential client calls you, you say after the first sentence or two, "Just in case we get cut off Mr. / Miss. X, let me get your name, address, phone number and email." Capture every potential's information so you CAN get back to them and follow up.

If the caller is viable at all as a client, that same day, you or your admin must Fed-Ex, OVERNIGHT a package to the potential, including your book, a sheet of testimonials, and a personal letter from you. Yes, it will cost $10-$20 per potential. So freaking what? This is NOT expensive.

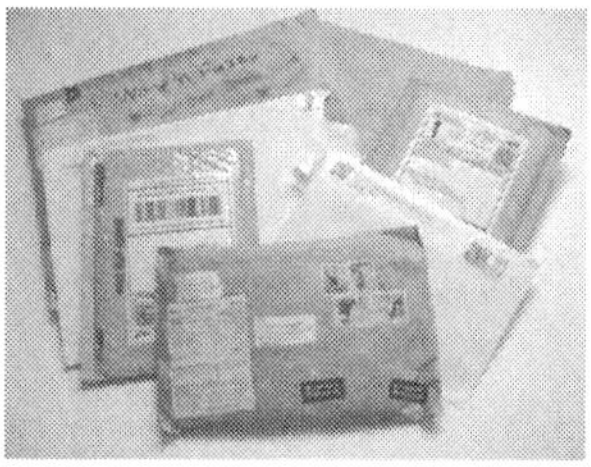

If you do this for 10 potential clients a month, it is $150-$200 a month. When this earns you 1-2 or more extra clients, is it expensive then?

Why does this work so well? Normally, a potential client will call several attorneys to evaluate. Most will sound about the same; maybe one sounds better than the other, but hiring an attorney requires thought, reflection, and bank-account checking, nevermind <u>trust and belief that they've found "the right one"</u>.

The next day they get your package in the mail.

The potential says, "Oh, I remember that guy! He wrote a book? Wow. Impressive. Here are testimonials from people who've hired him and obviously believed in him. He's credible. People seem to really like this guy. He has even taken the time to write me a personal letter and Fed-Ex this package to me and spend money!"

Compare the emotional, logical, and influential impact your package will have to other law firms that just call the person 3 or 4 times to harrass them by phone. This separates you from the pack and gives you tremendous authority, credibility and celebrity.

<u>Scenario #2:</u> You do a phone consult with a potential, just like before. Everything's going well and they make an appointment with you 2+ days in the future. Do the exact same thing as in Scenario #1. Overnight the book, testimonials and a letter from you. Follow the same script: "Just in case we get cut off Mr. X, let me get your name, address, phone number and email."

<u>Here's what else you or your admin should say</u>: "I look forward to meeting you next Friday. In preparation for our meeting, I am Fed-Ex'ing you some very useful and important information in the mail. You'll receive it in the next day or so, so be on the lookout! It may ease your mind about what will happen moving forward. It is a book I wrote on the area of law you are having problems with. Even if we aren't a fit and don't work together, you'll be well-prepared to hire the right attorney for you."

Even though they've made an appointment with you, guess what's happening in the potential's world?

They hang up and talk to friends and family about their upcoming appointment with you. Well-meaning friends and family cast major doubt on your decision. They remind you that your Uncle Bobby is a lawyer and can do the job a lot cheaper.

Meanwhile, other attorneys are calling, harassing seducing, lowballing, emailing and pitching them.

There's a lot of noise and major "buyer's remorse" going on.

Your book, testimonials and letter are going to cut through all the noise, fear, uncertainty, and doubt.

There is the fear of meeting you in person; the fear of dealing with the legal issues themselves; the doubt cast by friends and family over your decision; your doubt in yourself that you aren't guilty and shouldn't give up. Then, voila! Just in time, they get your package in the mail and the dial on the chorus of doubts gets turned way, way down.

Your no-show becomes a fo' sho.

(Bad pun - fo' sho means "for sure")

Scenario #3: Initial phone consult leads to booking an office appointment, and the potential actually shows up for their in-office appointment… **but** they give an excuse for not retaining you right then and there… and now they're about to walk out the door - what do you do?

You've spent a lot of time, effort, $500 to $800 in marketing money (on average) getting this potential to come to your office and hear your initial consultation! *Don't Forget That.* About to walk out the door, the potential may tell you: "I'll be back;" or "I need to speak to my wife;" or "I have to think about it;" or even worse: "You're too expensive;" or "I don't have the money" or "I can't afford it".

Before they walk out that door, hand them the book you wrote, a sheet of testimonials, and a letter from you, and tell them the following:

"I want you to have a resource that'll help you in your decision. Here's a book I authored about this particular area of law."

"The reason I wrote it is to fully answer any un-asked or lingering questions people have about {subject area}."

"It may be extremely useful and informative for you, and funny enough, it often inspires people to think of more questions."

"Even if you decide we're not a fit and can't work together, this will help you make a more informed decision."

Compare the effect of giving the prospect your book, testimonials, and stick letter versus:

"Bye, bye, see you later. I hope to hear from you soon."
You're reading this book this very moment.
What effect is it having on YOU?

You now know 3 areas of your sales funnel where you should use the physical book you authored and why.

Re-cap of the Benefits of a Physical Book and Credibility Package:

- Retain a MUCH higher percentage of clients.

- Increase your authority, credibility and celebrity in the eyes of potential clients.
- Retain a higher QUALITY of client. Tire kickers and cheapskates will weed themselves out.
- Cut down on "no shows, be-backs, call-you-later's, talk-to-my-wife's, got to think about it, I don't have enough money", etc.
- Command higher fees for your work due to your elevated status vs. other attorney competitiors.

How would you like to retain more clients by spending just a fraction of a normal marketing budget?

Tighten up your sales funnel, and you just might get off the treadmill of chasing more and more marketing channels.

Now, Let's Talk About EXCUSES Why 99% of Attorneys Sadly WON'T Author a Book or Tighten Up Their Sales Funnel

The first few bullshit excuses I call the 'Goldie Locks Syndrome':

#1 - "The book is too thin. No one is going to read it. It's too flimsy." A 1 hour Q&A interview-style recorded, transcribed call turns into a 55-65 page, 5 1/2" x 8-1/2" glossy cover paperback book.

#2 - "The book is too thick. No one will ever read it." Wait a minute! I thought the book was too thin and flimsy – now someone else is complaining it's too THICK?

#3 - "Nobody's gonna read this. People don't read anymore, they just look at their smartphones and ipads." (psst! Aren't you READING this book this very moment? People read what interests them.

Happy Fact: Merely the act of the potential holding the book in their hands and thumbing through it for 5 seconds gives you 90% of the benefit of authoring the book.

Maybe 1 in 100 people will read the entire book. But a vast majority will at least thumb through it, become impressed, read the testimonials, thumb through the first few and last few pages.

Some will scan the table of contents and read a particularly interesting or relevant chapter.

Let go of the Goldie Locks Syndrome. Too thick, too thin, too this, too that. This stuff WORKS.

...MORE BS Excuses

"The book should be written as a regular textbook-style book, not an interview. ***It must be professional.***"

People want information, not a textbook. They won't tolerate being bored to death. People want to be entertained, and a boring, "professional", dry book filled with legalese is not going to interest anyone.

These books are in interview format because it's far more interesting to read than textbook format. Who wants to be preached to? People have questions that demand an answer in a way they can easily understand. That's what the interview format does – **it recreates the back and forth interaction of an initial consult by phone or in person.**

What happens if your book addresses all the common questions potentials relentlessly ask you, over and over, for the past 5, 10 or 20 years? The book will inform, entertain, and instill a sense of gratitude, respect, and awe of your knowledge and abilities – **you'll become the obvious choice to hire, price be damned.**

...Even MORE Excuses

"It costs too much to do a book." Did you know that most companies charge $10,000 - $100,000 to publish your book, nevermind helping you CREATE IT!

In the spirit of making this accessible to hard-working attorneys who aren't rolling in the dough, yes, it'scurrently way underpriced, ranging from $1,500 - $2,500, including 100 physical copies, shipped to your doorstep.

At this price, even if you only retain ONE MORE CLIENT than you would have, the book pays for itself.

Your book will last you at least 2 years, and/or until the laws significantly change; you can always update it.

Excuse #5,837: "I don't have the time to author a book." If you don't have an hour to spend speaking the book and an hour to do final corrections, then you don't have time to read this book, either, so just give up and pray for a miracle.

Avoiding an SEO / Website Hostage Situation with Your Vendors

Forget about just being "burned"...
...many an attorney has been taken hostage by their web person, SEO guy, or marketing firm, pay per click company, or Google® Maps Optimizer.

I'm not exaggerating, and
<u>no, this isn't a ridiculous statement</u>.

I've heard dozens of horror and hostage stories.

Does this sound familiar?
A law firm hires a company to build them a website, and the company says it will take 3 months. An entire year passes, filled with excuses, delays, and utter lies, and the website goes live on the internet, only 70% finished. You paid the web designer thousands only to end up with a piece of junk that's not even fully functional.

Here's a common hostage situation:
You sign a 1 or 2 year contract with an SEO and website design company. You're promised a new website, and SEO work for the contract term. You're told that you won't have to blog and that all the content for your website will be written by the company's "in-house professional staff".
How will progress be tracked? By the company's "proprietary client dashboard".

Who will handle your account? An overly happy, sunshine up-your-ass-blowing account rep who puts **!!! Exclamation Marks!!!** at the end of each sentence in their emails and WRITES IN ALL CAPS.

Here's what you DON'T KNOW... Many of these companies put your website up on a domain name that *they own*, NOT YOU.

Let's say you practice criminal defense in Minneapolis, Minnesota and the company you've contracted with sets up your website onMinnesotaCrimDefense.com (disclaimer: not a real website at the time of this publication)

Scary Fact: **90% of 400+ attorneys I've spoken to don't even know if they own their own domain name.**

I find this amazing, scary, tragic, and worth mentioning. Don't you?

So if you don't own your own domain name, you certainly don't own any of the articles, images (i.e. 'content'), web traffic, or anything else associated with the website, **YET YOU ARE PAYING FOR IT,** doesn't that seem like a future hostage situation, just begging to happen?

Once your contract term is up with these website terrorists, its hostage situation time. You've paid thousands of dollars to have them design, supposedly SEO your website, fill it with content, and now your contract is nearing its end.

Unless you agree to the terrorists' new terms and payment amounts, what recourse do you have? Stop paying and the lights get turned off. The sign on the door gets changed to the next sucker and you're left with absolutely nothing.

Oh, but don't worry – you can always "buy out" your contract so you can own the content and maybe even the domain name for just $12,000 - $15,000. No problem at all!

Any account you do not own and control access to is a future liability, headache, nightmare, and hostage situation.

Own every single blessed account that you use in your business. Own your domain name, your hosting, your Google+, Google Places, Google Analytics. Own your phone numbers, own everything.

How should you interact with your vendors? Give them access to your accounts with a login and password. Then, at 2 in the morning while you're lying in bed, tossing and turning and having nightmares about not getting enough clients, you can grab your iPad or laptop, login, change the passwords, and go back to sleep a happy lawyer.

The next day, if your vendor freaks out, they can do nothing to hurt you. If your vendor says nothing for weeks or a month, then that's proof positive the vendor isn't even doing anything for you, just draining you of your money.

The Mechanics of Domain Names & Hosting

The place where you buy your domain name is called your "**Domain Name Registrar".** Buying a domain name for a year is dirt cheap, currently costing about $15. Instead of buying a domain name for 1 year and worrying about renewing it, I would spend $60 and buy a domain name for 3-5 years.

Once you have a domain name, you have to **host it** somewhere. A hosting company takes the files that make up your website - and that's what your website "is" –just a bunch of computer files–and putsthem onto their computer servers that are connected to the internet. Then they hook up the networking plumbing to ensure your websites show up when someone puts in your domain name, or eventually, searches in Google, Yahoo or Bing and you show up in organic search results.

Usually your domain name registrar will also host your website. If not, there are tons of hosting companies out there.

Hosting isn't expensive, either, and runs about $20 a month.You don't want to go with the cheapest, crappiest hosting because it's not worth it. Middle of the road, $20 a month, is fine for almost every attorney I've talked to. Some like hostgator.com and almost everyone knows Go Daddy, Liquid Web and Rackspace. There are a lot of places you can get hosting.

What is Content?

Any articles, pictures, captions, videos or other consumable information on your website is called "content."

Your Content is Intellectual Property and can have substantial value. Don't Shortchange it.

Beware of content being created for you by 3rd party companies, article writers or video companies. Just like not owning your domain name or hosting or any other account, you must make sure you get signed releases from any content writers, videographers, or photographers giving you 100% unrestricted use of the content they create for you.

Doesn't matter if you paid for it - make sure to get the rights to it all, in writing, or you will be headed for trouble down the road.

Common Content Horror Story

Let's say you have a 2 year contract with a certain company. Your contract stipulates that you're renting the content – the web company creates it on your behalf, yet they own it.

Near contract's end, you decide you want to change providers or stop using this company. Your account rep says, "You have to pay us $10,000 to buy and keep the rights to your content and the content itself, otherwise, we have no choice but to take it all down."

How would you like to wake up to a skeleton website? A useless, stripped domain? The entire year of trying to get ranked in Google and get web visitors will be gone because your content will be gone. Within about a week, all your visitors from Google, Yahoo and Bing will go to zero because your website is now empty.

...and the best part? **You're legally plagiarizing your own content** if you copy and keep it on your website. You'll have to write all new stuff. Talk about getting screwed over.

Hostage situations like this come about because attorneys don't realize that their website becomes an asset over time that can be worth a LOT of MONEY.

Don't Overlook This: All parts of your profile, presence and visibility on the web- such as Facebook, Twitter, LinkedIn, Google Adwords Pay Per Click, Google Maps, Google Local, Google Plus, Google Analytics, Yahoo, Bing, Yellowbook, YellowPages, CitySearch, Judy's Book, MerchantCircle, Yelp, AVVO, FindLaw, etc, you must have the log in and password for every single account.

The same hostage situation can and will happen when the time comes if you don't. Tie down all potential loose cannons NOW.

As an attorney, you know relationships often start out beautiful and rosy and then turn to hatred and bickering when parties start disagreeing. Word to the wise: (and you attorneys SHOULD be wise) Own everything- all logins and passwords. Then you can lock out anyone you want at any time and control all that is said about you on the web.

Otherwise, you're headed for disaster andit's *your own fault.*

WHY YOUR WEBSITE CAN BE SO MUCH MORE THAN YOU EVER THOUGHT POSSIBLE

Your website is your intellectual property. You spend thousands of dollars and often years to develop it. It is something that can stay with you for years and it is your asset and you have to treat it as one.
You can also be held liable if your content is not bar-compliant or misleading. You really have to take care of your web presence and your website to ensure you own and benefit from it in every sense of the word.

One of the most exciting benefits of owning and building a good website is it's ability to attract and bring you potential clients.

Did you know?It's not uncommon for a properly cared for, curated, SEO'd, and content-rich attorney website to CONSISTENTLY ATTRACT 3, 5, even 8 potential clients a month. Month in and month out.

How much can your website be worth to you?
Let's say you're a DUI / DWI attorney and you charge $2,500 for a low-end, 1st time DUI case with no trial needed.

Your website is 2 years old, has been SEO'd and content-filled from day one, and is now getting 75 unique visitors from Google / Yahoo / Bing a day.

On average, you get 24 calls a month from potential clients and convert 15%, which is about 4 clients a month.

4 clients/month * $2,500/client = $10,000 a month gross retention revenue.

$10,000 / month * 12 months/yr = $120,000 a year gross revenue from your website alone.

Expenses? Your SEO company is a good one, and they charge a fair amount → $1,000 a month ($12k/yr).

Your website now nets you $120k - $12k = $108k a year

$108,000 a year from your website.
How do ya like dem' assets?

...and when you go to retire and either sell your practice, sell out to a partner or close your doors?

You now have an asset that is very reasonably valued at 1x yearly net earnings of $108,000.

"...and that's the triple truth, Ruth." - Samuel Jackson's character in the movie, 'Do the Right Thing'.

WHY GETTING ON PAGE 1 OF GOOGLE IS A MEANINGLESS WASTE OF TIME

I'm not saying this just to be contrarian or shock you, but if you've been sold on the collective fantasy that getting to be #1 in Google for a few, juicy, select keywords is the key to internet riches, then you're on a wild goose chase with an unhappy end.

Getting to #1 in Google for a few keywords is a meaningless waste of time, and I'm going to explain why using my personal experience, not theory or fantasy.

Every attorney thinks people mostly search a few, coveted, particular phrases in Google and it's just not true. Some of the dream attorney keywordsI've heard are:

- New York City auto accident lawyer
- Dallas DWI attorney
- Probation violation attorney
- Orlando sex crime lawyers
- Los Angeles criminal defense

So how do I knowthat chasing these particular keywords and others like them is a waste of time?

I grew myDUIattorney.org starting from ZERO unique Google searches. The website is a group attorney advertisement where people arrested for drunk driving nationwide can enter in their information that is directly passed on to a DUI / Criminal Defense attorney in or near their zip code.

As of February 2013 Google sends 1,100+ UNIQUE searchers a day (33,000+ visitors a month).

myDUIattorney.org has helped deliver over 35,000 DUI leads since mid-2010.

Would YOU call that successful?

Go ahead and Google the website nowadays using various fantasy keywords and you probably won't see it show up in Google search - so how the heck does it consistently get 33,000+ visits for many months now?

About 18 months ago the site used to be #1 in Google nationally for "DUI attorney" and "DUI lawyer".

Guess how many Google searches came from being on top of the world for the juiciest 2 terms in the DUI world? Not hundreds, not thousands; but about 8 searches a day for each of those 2 keywords. **Think about that.**

We got 33,000 searches a month. 16 of them were from the dream keywords everyone fantasizes about.

Guess how many different keywords made up the 33,000 searches a month?

➔ 25,794 Different Keywords

Just think about what that means. If only a few keywords were important out of 33,000 searches, we would have seen maybe 500 different keywords. Instead, over 80% of all searches were UNIQUE and DIFFERENT.

And the searches were NOT what you think they'd be - they were all kinds of crazy sentences people type in when they've been arrested for DUI, such as:

- Arrested in San Francisco and blew .11 now what
- 2nd DUI will I go to jail
- Cop said I failed breathalyzer but I wasn't drunk
- Best attorneys in Milwaukee who take payment plans on drunk driving cases

So you tell me, how important is it to be on the top of the first page of Google for any one particular keyword or a small set of keywords? It is a meaningless waste of time. I proved it.

Google themselve have said: "50% of all searches on any given day are UNIQUE" – i.e. they have NEVER BEEN TYPED IN BEFORE.

But what does Google know? **They only control 84%+ of all search engine traffic.** *They only made $46 BILLION in 2012* from people googling endless billions of different keyword phrases.

Not only are the precious, bejeweled, coveted, wet dream keywords everyone fantasizes about not bringing in very many searches from Google, no one, not even the people searching themselves, know what keywords you SHOULD be on Page 1 of Google for.

So how the devil do you successfully do SEO?

Probably no other topic drives me crazier than to hear attorney after attorney crying about their competitor being above them in Google for one or two glorious keywords they're lusting after. I hear this garbage every single day, and it's a wild goose chase – a waste of time.

Oh, and by the way, what makes it even worse is that you'd be hard pressed to find ANY SEO COMPANY out there that doesn't say, "We'll get you to the top of

Google. We'll get you on page 1 for 10 keywords. We guarantee you'll get in Google Maps, or appear for this keyword."

It's fake science, complete bullshit, a false messiah, a wasted journey. 99% of attorney's are misinformed about page one of Google, but not you, dear reader. Not anymore ☺.

Why Haven't You Heard About This Before? Is There a Google Conspiracy?

You've gotta go pretty deep into SEO to understand how search behavior truly works.

I've spent 3+ years attending marketing conferences, studying Google and the other search engines, talking to experts in the field, and pursuing my passion for SEO and marketing in general to learn what I'm telling you.

99% of SEO companies are there to sell you the red or blue widget off the shelf, real results be damned. **Selling page 1 of Google for 10 top keywords is sexy - the truth is not.**

Still skeptical? Go ahead and call my live attorney references listed on SpeakEasyMarketingInc.com or call me and I'll give you 20 more attorneys to talk to. My attorney clients are tremendously diversified SEO-wise, and content-wise, and are getting calls every single day from potential clients. Of course, some more than others, but some of my top clients get 100+ Google searches a DAY, which makes their phones ring every single day with potential clients.

All the while, other attorneys are starving to death and chasing the same worthless, phantom keywords.

Here's WHY 50% of all searches are new and why a few, lame keywords are a tiny minority of what people search:

When you *"Google"* something, you're compressing your entire problem, your emotions, and your thoughts into a few words inside a Google search box. Google searches and searchers are as different and varied as there are people in the world.

Everyday people are searching just for stuff that no one is nor CAN directly SEO for, because the searchers themselves are making up their search queries on the fly, depending on Google to give them the answer they're looking for from a sentence fragment or laymen's method of compressing their desire into a few words.

Another fact: Over 95% of people never make it past the first page of Google when they'researching, so yes it IS vital to be on the 1st page of Google for the "right" search terms…

…but for 10,000 keywords that are thematically related to what you offer, not word-for-word specific.

Think about the keywords you want to be on Page 1 of Google for, and imagine each of them as a dandelion, with the specific dream keyword as the small seeded-center of the dandelion. The hundreds of related keywords to your specific keyword are the white fluffy hairs and strands of the dandelion – they make up a diffuse cloud – a THEME that you want to show up in Google for.

How to Get Onto the 1st Page of Google for 10,000 Different Keywords:

The answer is content, content and more content – i.e. words found in articles. Google can't read images yet. Google can't translate videos yet or read Flash programming language (fancy moving graphics on websites). **Google's search engine ranking algorithm reads and relies upon TEXT – words, phrases, sentences, and articles.**

Example #1: Someone is searching to find information on the consequences of refusing a breath test in Boston,

Massachusetts, on a 2nd DUI offense. Chances are you will show up for that search on Page 1 of Google if you're a Boston, Massachusetts attorney, (it's also where you practice DUI defense specifically) and you've written an article specifically about breath test refusals and their consequences for 1st vs. multiple DUI offenses.You also have to have a strong website that has many relevant links from other good websites to yours. (more on that shortly)

Example #2: Someone is searching for help with a shoplifting charge in Austin, Texas. They had a prior 4 years ago and want to know the look back period and if they'll have mandatory jail time on the 2nd offense. Well you want to make sure, as an attorney in that area who handles theft crimes, that you have an article that talks about that as specifically as possible, and again, a site with high link popularity.

Now imagine if you built up 200 different articles on your website on every aspect of the law that you practice; you adequately cover all frequently asked questions, subject areas, penalties, defenses, and even minutiae of various situations?

You'll start to appear on page 1 of Google (and even at the top of many 1st pages of Google) for THOUSANDS of different keywords or more, NOT just 10 or 20.

You won't know what they are and neither will anyone else until people actually start searching and your website shows up in Google search.

If you install Google Analytics (a free program that shows you what people type in to find your website thru their search engine) **you'll start to see what searchers are ACTUALLY typing in to find you** - and yes, you'll be very surprised.

With many articles on your site and more added over time, you'llstart getting a lot of Google searches every day. It's definitely possible to build up to 100+ organic searches a day for a local attorney after about 12-18 months worth of SEO.

Google Analytics

This many searches will get your phone ringing every single day with potential clients, and yes, some of my attorney clients have been patient enough to let me grow their websites to this level and beyond.

These guys are kicking ass in Google, and the most beautiful thing of all? They're succeeding below the radar, because their websites aren't showing up at the top of Google for the worthless dream keywords everyone cries out for.

Just like with myDUIattorney.org and other successful websites, **out of 100 searches a day, 90+ will be *different.***

And if you think this phenomenon of the "Long Tail" occurs just with SEO, you'd be surprised to learn it happens with Google Adwords (Pay Per Click), Google Maps, and in every single area of online advertising where people search for answers.

ONLY diverse content (lots of articles on every aspect of your practice areas) will get you on Page 1 of Google for thousands of keywords.

Several hundred articles on your website, each of which address specific concerns or a tight theme of concerns is what you need to have a successful site.

Here's an example of the articles possible (and needed) in theDUI defense world:

- Common misconceptions people have about their arrest
- Unintentional mistakes people make during and after their arrest that negatively affects their case and their potential outcomes
- If you fail Field Sobriety Tests, are you doomed to be convicted?

- What happens if you refuse the breath or blood test once you've been arrested?
- What are the driver's license consequences of a DUI arrest and/or conviction?
- How do penalties, both criminal and administrative, escalate for 2nd, 3rd, or multiple offenders?
- Why hire a lawyer who focuses on DUI vs. a general criminal defense lawyer or public defender?

Here's an example of the articles possible (and needed) in theCar Accident World:

- Am I obligated to provide a statement to the other party's insurance adjuster? They're calling me off the hook.
- Why not immediately seeing a doctor and documenting your injuries may hurt your ability to collect
- Common misconceptions people have about car accidents and lawsuits to "get the money they deserve"
- If I am in a collision with an underinsured or uninsured motorist, does that mean I can't collect any compensation?

If I'm searching for information about my DUI arrest, my domestic violence charge, my auto accident, my possible bankruptcy, etc, and…

…I come to your site and immediately see you specifically addressed my problem or question, I am calling <u>YOU</u>, not the 500 other attorneys who have the same, boilerplate gobbledygook content on their sites, stuffed full of keywords.

Does the following sound familiar?

A Los Angeles DUI is a serious offense. You want to hire an experienced, aggressive Los Angeles DUI attorney to fight your DUI charges in Los Angeles. Oh, and by the way, did I mention "Los Angeles DUI 10 times in the first freaking paragraph? Does this make for informative reading? No. Google's search engine knows it's garbage filler as well.

Lastly, the content strategy I've laid out here is what works in Google today in 2013, and it is not going to change anytime soon. Google demands unique, informative, relevant content, so playing by their rules only benefits you.

So please, don't be a lemming. Don't be lured onto the rocks by the siren song of 10 garbage keywords on Page 1 of Google. Go for 10,000 keywords instead.

Giant Swiss Cheese or Huge Spider Web - How Visitors ACTUALLY InteractWith your Website

Bad websites look like the movie set of an Old West town. You have a painted, landscaped, beautiful front façade / front yard / **HomePage**.

But as soon as you walk behind the front façade, you see the back and sides are completely empty; they're held up by a wood frame of 2x4's.

Real websites look like 3-D spider webs or a gigantic wheel of Swiss cheese with lots of holes in it.

➔ Visitors search "the web" (pun intended) and may be caught in the kill zone of your spider website from any strand, in any direction.

➔ Information hungry mice (Google searchers) can enter in through hundreds of holes in your wheel of Swiss Cheese.

Most folks think that all website visitors enter through their homepage, which is a serious error. This leads to spending way too much time on your homepage and neglecting all the other pages of your website.

Did you know that each page of your website will preferentially appear in Google for certain keywords? If you have a page about Domestic Violence penalties, but your website contains pages on Theft Crimes, DUI, Weapons Offenses, etc, and someone Googles: *"will I have mandatory jail for a 1st domestic violence charge"*, Google will show THAT particular page in its search results, NOT your homepage.

Makes sense, doesn't it? **Your domestic violence page is the most relevant to that person's search, NOT your homepage, so Google shows THAT page.**

When you realize that every single page of your website can and will be landed on by people searching Google, you no longer have a website - you have a spider web or giant wheel of Swiss cheese - choose your favorite image.

Why does this happen? Understand that if Google didn't do a damn good job matching what people search for with the most relevant search results, Yahoo or Bing would be king.

Instead, Google controls 80% of all searches and makes over $46 billion a year from search marketing. So Google knows what the heck it is doing.

Now do you see how you can get to Page 1 of Google for thousands of keyword searches? Each page of your website has a chance to appear in the 1st page of Google for the theme of keywords it has on it - the content that it has.

So your homepage can be beautifully optimized and compelling, but if the other pages look like crap, you have a big problem.

Every page of your website has to:

- Be compelling, informative, and straight to the point
- Immediately answer a searcher's question, without having to hunt around for the answer
- Look pleasing to the eye and easily navigable
- Pull visitors deeper into your site and engage them, not have them bounce (click the 'back button' to leave the site) without visiting another 2nd or 3rd page.

Not only do you want to have many articles that discuss all the details of your practice areas, you have to ADD to your content over time and grow it. Mice don't want a small, moldy piece of cheese and won't bite. Flies won't fly into a tiny web of breakable strands. Google won't favor either.

Keep these pictures in mind. The sooner you can see your website for how it truly gets visitors using these two visuals, the better you can craft your strategy of attracting, trapping and retaining mice, flies or potential clients.

How to Attract, Educate, Show Credibility & Authority, and Compel Potentials to Call Your Office or Fill In Your Contact Us Form

Here are some specific strategies I use to get my attorney client websites more visitors, make the visits stickier, last longer, and compel more potentials to call and eventually retain:

#1: Create and Offer a book(or guide)visitors can download for free that will educate them on a specific practice area or topic. Examples of this can be found on my attorney client websites, with titles such as: "Milwaukee DUI Arrest? Useful Info Revealed That May Help Your Case"

Your free book / guide acts as bait when people visit your website, shows them your authority and credibility, and offers them a non-threatening way to learn more without calling you and being pitched.

Whatever page they land on or navigate to, they can grab your free content, take it with them and read it; and then come back, call and potentially hire you.

#2: Write tons of content / articles on all kinds of specifics. Show your site visitors you know exactly what's bugging them and how you can help. Let's say someone is searching whether they are going to jail for a 2nd time DUI charge where they blew above a .15. If you have an article that talks about that, they're going to think: "Wow, this attorney has an answer that addresses **MYPARTICULAR SITUATION**. I am going to call."

#3: Have a related articles widget on every single article page, to give people a logical way to further explore your site and go deeper to find the answers they're looking for. This helps pull people deeper into the site. Let's say someone searches Google for: "failed field sobriety test."

You should have related articles that are titled:

- If you fail the field sobriety tests, are you automatically guilty?
- Medical conditions that affect field sobriety tests
- Can you refuse to perform FSTs?

The related articles widgets help visitors spend more time, and build more appreciation for what you offer and make you stand out when "being aggressive" won't. This is more likely to lead to a phone call to you.

#4: Make sure the navigation makes sense on your site and visitor can look up and see immediately where they want to go, without getting trapped in a certain area of your website.

If I'm on an article page, I want to be able to look up and see that attorney's profile. If I want to jump to another section, I can quickly click and go right there no matter what page I'm on.

#5: Visitors want to see testimonials to build trust, and they must be able to find them instantly. Make your testimonials visible everywhere on your site so people get reinforcement that you do a good job; that you're a good attorney and others have hired you and have had good outcomes.

Testimonials silently imply that YOU should hire this person - they speak very loudly in your defense.

#6: Phone number, email, physical address and office hours are very important to have everywhere. You never know where people will enter your site, and one of the first and last things they''ll do once they decide they need help is look for your phone number, address or email to contact you. Why make it hard for people to contact you? Why make them expend energy to search for your info?

So next time you pass a spider web in the office or eat a piece of Swiss Cheese, think of your website, you'll think twice ☺

SEO IN ITS UNDERWEAR - CONTENT & LINKS IS 90% OF WHAT MATTERS

****Make sure to review 'why getting on the 1st page of Google is a meaningless waste of time'and 'how a successful website looks like a spider web or gigantic wheel of Swiss cheese'.****

For attorneys, successful search engine optimization (SEO) has 2 main pillars: content and links.

To begin, Google now has made it such that ***no one on earth can rush SEO results any more***. No one can get you on the first page of Google overnight. Getting 30, 50, or even 100+ unique visitors a day using SEO takes 6 months, sometimes 1 year.

> ➔ Anyone that promises quick page 1 of google ranking is lying to you, plain and simple. ←

Google's algorithm has gotten so sophisticated, complicated and good at fighting spam that Zeus himself couldn't rush the process.

6-12 months of SEO can get your website to the 30-100 unique daily visitor level, which puts you in range of having your phone ring multiple times a week or possibly every single day with potential clients.

Impatient attorneys often think, at this point: "Why bother? I don't have time for this. I don't want to wait 6-12 months!"

Why Bother Doing SEO, Long Term?

Think of SEO as getting yourself in cardiovascular shape – i.e. committing to regular gym workouts. It gives you long term benefits just like working out and building muscle, and the good thing is its results stay with you.

Unlike buying leads, running Google Adwords (pay per click), direct mail, banners, or other fast-response advertising, the day you stop SEO, you're not going to wake up the next day with no muscle tone and a cholesterol-clogged heart needing a quadruple bypass.

The moment you stop any of the above marketing methods or stop paying, the lights get shut off, and so does your phone and email leads. Gone, like telling a stripper you have no money. Gone without even so much as a smile.

Well done SEO can stay with you for a long time, and even if you stop, it does not fade instantly. I recommend you do it forever, so long as you're profiting from it - i.e. you're making an ROI from your spend on it.

If the person doing SEO for you is doing their job properly, you'll experience an evolution from monthly expense to breakeven, to profit center over 6-12 months.

When SEO is done right, it starts to pay for itself, by attracting enough phone calls and emails from visitors to your website (that you must still convert) to retained clients that pay you.

...As you continue building, SEO turns into a profit center, reliably getting you 4, 5, 6, maybe even 10 retained clients a month. Now the letters S-E-O **become ROI** and there's no reason to stop, unless you don't understand basic math.

Does SEO Provide Quality Potential Clients or Just Tire Kickers and Time Wasters?

SEO is the carnival barker that gets people to your website - into the tent, and seated in front of the show. Unlike a salaried promoter, it's there to work for you day in and day out; continuously getting you clients.

Why does SEO bring high quality clients? Because people have to SEARCH Google, Yahoo &/or Bing, and take initiative to find you. Doesn't sound like a tall hill to climb, but effort is effort – they have to chase you, not you chasing them with your advertising.

As you well know, potential clients have many questions, and nowadays, people 'Google' everything. It starts with the search – a list of websites come up in search results. Each listing is, in fact, a tiny advertisement that looks like this:

Arrested for Shoplifting in Paramus, NJ? Call 201-555-1111
www.nj-criminal-lawyer-smith.com/shoplifting
Don't think shoplifting is a 'no-big-deal' crime. A conviction
may prevent you from being hired for many jobs. Call today.

Searchers quickly scan the ads and click on one that catches their eye and interest. Now the visitor lands on your website. (Remember, they may not land on your homepage!)

What's next? The visitor eyeballs your content – what's written, a picture or two, and decides within a few seconds if what they're searching for is matched by what's displayed on your website.

No match, no call, or perhaps more searching.Fail to compel visitors to read more or call you? A quick click of the back button takes them back to search results, and you've lost them, for now.

See all the effort and steps involved in someone **SEARCHING** for your information vs. you advertising to them on TV, a bus stop, billboard, or other means?

A well-written and presented, and SEO'd website lies in wait, attracting visitors and compelling them to become educated and call you - this is why SEO-based visitors tend to be higher quality potential clients - they've self-screened and only the more highly motivated ones will call or email.

Why Bother SEO'ing to Only Please Google? What About Yahoo, Bing, Ask, and the Other Search Engines?

You may be annoyed having to go through this whole rigmarole to please Google, but Google controls over 80% of all searches. Would you rather focus on 20% of the pie vs. 80% I didn't think so, so don't focus on Yahoo and Bing. Focus on Google and the other search engines will start showing your website, too. Sorry - it's time to let your dysfunctional love affair with Google Search begin.

What's The Process of "SEO'ing" a Website and Pleasing Almighty (Good) Google?

It starts with your mini ads that appear in Google search results (as I showed you previously). For each page of your website, you should take time to customize and a compelling ad (called a title and meta description tag) for each page of your website as you build and add to it.

The next goal of SEO is to optimize your website itself and make it 'Google friendly' or 'Google compliant'. There are myriad ways to do this, but one way is to structure your site so visitors who enter from any landing page can navigate quickly wherever they need to go on your site - i.e. no dead ends or ratholes where people can get stuck in an area without an obvious way of getting out.

You also want to structure your site so people: hit a landing page, are drawn further into the site, and compelled to click on at least one more page. This helps minimize the percent of visitors bouncing off your site after just seeing 1 page. (Called Bounce Rate - an indicator of how engaging your site is in Google's eyes) Surprisingly, a good bounce rate is 50% for some pages and as high as 95% for others.

Always keep in mind that **your home page is not where** all visitors enter, as discussed in the Swiss cheese and spider web section. Remember, visitors come in through the windows, the basement, the side door, the attic. They come in from every direction and on every possible page, depending on the content of that page.Shoplifting searches will land people on your shoplifting page. Sex crime searches will land people on those pages. General inquiries may go to your FAQ or homepage.

Without being exhaustive, here's more that should be done: Set up Google maps; set up a site map; make sure you have terms and conditions, a disclaimer that by reading your site no attorney-client relationship is being created, and have a privacy policy.

All of these baseline boilerplate things need to be done to make your site Google compliant.

The home-grown, mistake-inspired checklist I use on my attorney clients' behalf has 80+ different line items to make sure a website is ready and optimized to show up in Google.

Here's a good idea: As you talk to different SEO companies, ask to see their checklist for onsite optimization (i.e. the stuff they do to get a site ready to show up SEO-wise in Google).

Note: Want to see my 80+ item checklist? Email or call me and I'll gladly share.

Once you've done on-site initial optimization -most of the work is upfront and only requires a small amount of maintenance from then on - we move to the heart of SEO.

The 2 Pillars of SEO – Content & Backlinks

The 2 pillars of SEO are content and links pointing to your site, both obtained continuously, at a somewhat steady pace, over time.

Content is articles, relevant pictures, video, audio, and downloadable versions of the same, all posted on your website. Google searches on words, the presence of videos, pictures, and audio. **95%+ of Google relies on TEXT**, so remember, content is vital, and words are king.

When you "google" something, you're typing in... WORDS.

When Google's algorithm pulls up relevant websites, you're now looking mainly at WORDS / TEXT.

When a Googler clicks on a website, remember, every single page of a website can be landed on by a visitor, not just the home page.

What are searchers faced with once they land on your site? Your website's CONTENT. Words, pictures, videos, audio.

What's Your Website's Content Look Like?

Imagine the typical criminal defense attorney's 20 page website that has cobwebs growing on it because it hasn't changed in years. None of the articles are new - the entire website is...static. These commonplace websites have an attorney profile page, a few pages of skeleton content, maybe a disclaimer, a contact us form, and not much else.

Now I want you to imagine that 90 pound weakling website shoved in the dirt by a 300 pound linebacker website made up of 300+ pages, containing 200 different articles on your various practice areas and the common questions and answers surrounding them.

A well-developed DUI website for instance, would contain articles on DUI charges and consequences for 1st time and multiple offenders, common defenses, breath testing & refusals, field sobriety tests; driver's license suspension consequences; post-conviction relief; probation types, lengths and violations, constitutional rights, victim impact panels, and more.

A broader criminal defense website would have articles on sex crimes; cybercrimes; robbery and assault; gun crimes; domestic violence; the different levels of misdemeanor versus felony crimes; juvenile criminal law; traffic offenses; theft crimes such as shoplifting, grand larceny and burglary, why hire a private attorney vs. a public defender, and more.

I'll give you zero guesses: which website, the weakling vs. the 6'5" linebacker - who will get all the girls?

People 'Google' thousands of different things daily, for millions of different questions plaguing them.

If you want to get 30, 50,or 100+ daily Google searches (which translate directly into phone calls and email inquiries from potential clients), can a cobweb-covered, moldy cheese website that hasn't been touched in a year have a snowball's chance in hell of getting there?

...or will the active, growing, changing, content-filled, and developing website with 200+ articles on it get there?

Before You Complain About Writing 200+ Articles, Videos, and Creating Content...

Read the section on the Attorney-Author-Authority-Process. In it, I teach you how to effortlessly speak 7,000+ words an hour by phone and fill up your website almost completely in about nine, 1-hour-long sessions.

The 2nd Pillar of SEO – Links From 3rd Party Websites

A hyperlink ('link') is a bit of blue, highlighted text with an underline that you can click that takes you to another webpage or website entirely. The clickable words that make up a link are called the link's anchor text or link text.

In Google's eyes, just like a high school popularity contest, Google favors more popular, more respected and more linked-to websites vs. orphans. Other sites show respect and **give an implied recommendation** to visit your site by linking to it. At first glance, the more to your website sitting on 3rd party websites, the more popular and stronger your site will be and the more it will show up on the fabled 1st Page of Google results for more keywords.

Here come the twists. Anytime someone searches for something, it's Google's job to seemingly instantly sift and sort thousands of websites and decide which site to show at the top of the 1st page, which one 2nd, then 3rd, ad infinitum.

How does Google do this? There's over 200 factors baked into its algorithm, but a MAJOR FACTOR is which sites have the most link popularity, and are therefore the most authoritative on the subject being searched AND relevant to it.

You'd be simplifying Google way too much to assume the sites with the highest number of links and the most content will automatically be ranked 1st.

The prize of playing by Google's rules? Showing up at the top of page 1 for thousands and thousands of searches.

Soliciting and harvesting links is the 2nd pillar SEO. Besides content, you want to get relevant, useful, quality links from other websites to show that yours is a worthwhile destination for searchers. Content without links gets you nowhere. Links without content get you nowhere.

In regards to links, don't think the more the merrier. In April-May 2012, Google slapped down millions of sites with their Panda and Penguin updates. They made it a lot harder for people to get credit for links that weren't "good", and many attorney websites lost ALL THEIR WEB TRAFFIC.

Here's how you judge if a link you want to get from another website to yours is worth asking for. The site has to be relevant to what you do, at least somewhat. Getting a link from a site about swimming pools is not going to be relevant to you as an attorney…Unless, they have an article on their site about swimming pool injuries and you are a personal injury attorney. Then, they link to you from that article, and the link makes sense to a human reviewer and to Google's algorithm and you get credit for it.

What kinds of sites and links meet the quality and relevance Google standard? Another attorney's link to you would be a highly relevant and desired link. If it's a beer site and you are a DUI lawyer, that may be relevant. A true crime website is also highly relevant to you. If it's a financial website, it might be relevant and it might not. You have to bridge the gap and make sure your link makes sense, by, for instance, talking about the financial consequences of being arrested for a crime, or losing your job or having a criminal record.

What Other Factors Make A Link Useful To You?

Make sure the site linking to you is authoritative and has been live on the web for a year or more - you don't want sites that were born yesterday. Older, more established sites are more authoritative. Sites with many quality links to them, or obviously authoritative websites (an extreme example is the State Bar website or other legal organizations) are desirable.

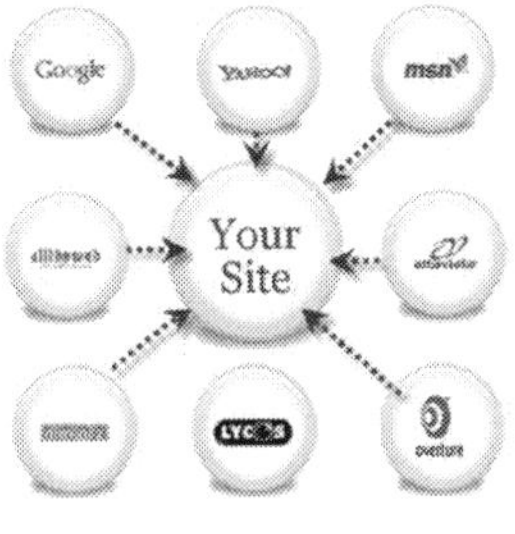

A link from a newspaper or top ranked attorney not in your field of practice are good to cultivate. The more authoritative the site linking to you, the more SEO Juice that link conveys and more traffic your site will attract from Google.

It's like a recommendation from your friend Joe versus a recommendation from the President of the United States. Which one conveys more authority to you? Which recommendation do you trust more highly? Google's thoughts, exactly.

Factors That Can Improve Or Hurt A Link

Run of Site Links - make sure when a site links to you, it doesn't link to you from every single page on that site - called a "run of site" link. Folks mistakenly think, "if a 100 page site links to me from every single page, I'll get 100 links." No, it doesn't work that way. Only 1 or 2 links from a given website give you Link Juice / SEO Juice. The others are redundant and can hurt you. If Google sees there are 100 links from the same site to you, they MAY devalue the link or hurt your search traffic because it makes no sense for a site to do this, and looks like spam, not true authority.

Link Text Keyword Stuffing / Redundancy - The link text itself, which is that blue underlined clickable text, can say different things. It can say "click here." It can say "Florida criminal defense lawyer." It can say "Learn about ABC Law Firm."

A lot of SEOs try to get the same link text over and over to your site. Let's say you want to be #1 for" Los Angeles personal injury lawyer." If every link they get you says, "Los Angeles personal injury lawyer" or "Los Angeles personal attorney", Google knows it's way too coincidental that 50 different sites would link to you using the same link text.

If you have 50 links, all with the same or similar link text, Mistress Google may crack her whip across your website's back and hurt your traffic.

You want to vary the link text while ensuring it makes sense, given the site it's coming from and the site it's linking to - i.e. your website.

Even if it's your name, the name of your firm, topic based, like: Dallas Dog Bite Attorney, or "click here for more info", all of those variations are expected and all are fine.

If a human being looks at your link profile or at any given link to your website, the acid test is: Does the link make sense or does it look like BS? If you pass the human viewer test and it makes sense, you will be fine.

Quality vs. Quantity Links – Who Wins?

<u>Note:</u>I paid $1,500 to the guy who does SEO for 1800 Flowers and the United States Patent and Trademark Office for a one day consult. He answered an important

question: "*If you get one good, relevant, authoritative link, is that equivalent to ten or 100 crappy, non-relevant links?"*

He said,*"A good, relevant, authoritative link can be worth as much as 1,000 crappy, garbage, non-relevant links."*

Now you understand the stupidity of SEO firms that say, "We'll get you 500 links a month for $500." These guys are incentivized to get you as many garbage links as possible to fulfill their agreement to get you 500 links.

Even better, you can beat them by getting 3 relevant links a month to your site instead of 500 garbage ones.

I paid a lot of money to learn this and here I am giving this information to you for free in this book, so pay attention.

SEO Requires Patience

Sorry to rain on your parade, but links take time and effort to find. They have to be vetted to make sure they benefit your site, not hurt it.

If you want to cut corners on content and links and try to blast your site to the top of Google, you'll wake up sooner or later with zero Google traffic, and a red, throbbing cheek where Google has slapped you with a penalty that's very difficult and time-consuming to undo.

How Long Does It
Really Take To Rank?
SEO

I've received plenty of calls from attorneys that cry, "Oh my God, we had 100 visitors a day and now we have none. Google killed us. What do we do to fix this?" Sorry buddy - when you anger the search engine gods, they unkindly cut you down.

Even though content and links take time, they certainly don't take FOREVER. Focus on both for 1 year, check up on your website's progress and you'll prosper just like my attorney clients do.

The reward of daily phone calls from potential clients and a consistent, 4-10 retained clients a month means a home-run ROI on your SEO. Your website then becomes a big time asset that can bring $100,000 a year or more in retention fees.

You now know WHAT to do, HOW to do it or at least monitor it's progress, so don't be an impatient crybaby and spend the next 12 months building yourself an asset.

SNAIL MAIL (AKA DIRECT MAIL OR JAILER MAILER) - YES, IT CAN GET YOU MANY RETAINED CLIENTS

Direct mail is literally getting an envelope and a stamp; putting a letter inside and mailing it through the U.S. Post Office, UPS or FedEx. Direct mail is also called "jail mail"or "snail mail."

In a world of Social Media Fanaticism, the "ancient tradition" of sending a letter in the mail is very effective. Did you realize that statistics say 65% of peoplehate getting e-mail and are completely overwhelmed by it?

No doubt you can't stand spam and you're in good company, because **94% of all e-mail sent is SPAM**. Not sure about you, but that amazes me to think what it would be like if spam ceased to exist.... Ahhhh...

On the contrary, 63% of people say they enjoy getting direct mail. They enjoy the experience of opening their mail, of getting a post card, or especially, a package.

Remember how you felt years ago when your grandparents sent you a Christmas card with money or even a care package?

A letter or package can delight or it can frighten, but at the end of the day, it causes a big-time emotional response, and THAT is what few other marketing methods can do as well.

Unless you're getting registered mail or an obivious bill, sorting through your mail can be an enjoyable experience, driven by curiosity.

Paper Mail Creates an Intimate Experience

Once you open a letter, it becomes a one-on-one experience. You're opening an envelope with your hands - it's a physical experience. You instinctively hold your breath for a moment until the envelope opens and you see what's inside.

There's noTwitteror Facebook pop ups. No way to click back to another 25 websites. There are no ads; none of the 99 distractions you feel on the internet.

How many windows do you have open on your computer from various web pages? Ever visit a web page and forget why you even went to it? Ever shake your head in frustration that you have a hard time paying attention to ANYTHING on the internet?

Compare that feeling to reading a paper letter on the toilet, or sitting back on your couch, reading. Feels like a bubble surrounds you and the letter you're reading and the outside worlds' sounds and events are shut out, if only for a minute.

How You Can Wield Direct Mail to Clobber Your Competitors

Ok, so you feel the romance of direct mail, but how is this useful to you as an attorney? Who wants to hear from YOU, an ATTORNEY? Yuck, right?

My favorite direct mail data guy, Mark, has been providing the names, home addresses, and charges of people recently arrested near to you for the past 8 years. His experience shows: **70% of criminal defense clients will procrastinate until 5 days or less before their court date**.

I bet you were thinking, "If you don't get 'em on the 1st or 2nd day, you'll never retain. They've all hired someone else by then." **NOT TRUE.**

Ask the man who has sent out 50,000 letters a month for the past 96 months what REALLY HAPPENS out there.

Moral of the story? If you're only hitting up potential clientsthe first 1-5 days, then giving up, ***you're missing***

out on 70% of the possible people that would otherwise retain you!!!

More chilling facts about attorney direct mail, if you're smart enough even to use it in the first place:

97% of mail sent by attorneys goes out 1 time ONLY, and the same day they get their potential client data.

Do you send multiple letters? Stats say only 3% do, because most folks mistakenly think 2nd, 3rd or 4th letters are not only "too expensive", but that everyone's already retained an attorney and it's too late.

Would you rather get 30% of the pie with a 1 time, day 1 mailer, or 100% of the pie with a 3-step mail sequence sent out over 1, 2 or 4 weeks?

There's huge opportunity in direct mail to get clients. I'm currently running direct mail for several attorney-clients.

One guy received 21 calls and retained 6 clients his first month doing it! **He spent $3,500 (because NY is the most expensive state to do it in, of course) and took in $18,400 in gross retainer fees.** NOT BAD, huh?

I've had to wrestle most lawyers to the ground to get them to try it, (ensuring their mail is State Bar-compliant). The results speak for themselves.

Supercharging Your Direct Mail Results

Most attorneys are afraid to even try direct mail, much less "push the envelope" (bad pun) to maximize it's return on investment.

In some cases, a plain letter in a white envelope with a stamp will serve you well, but there's a heck of a lot of tweaking, tracking and testing you have to do to (and should WANT to do) to push your results from 3x your money to possibly 10x your money or more.

How People Sort Their Mail

Did you realize that people sort their mail over the garbage can, mentally making a "keeper" pile of interesting stuff that must be opened now, a 2nd pile of essentials, like bills, and tossing the rest?

The first things to get opened and read areitemspeople think are personal, interesting, or evoke curiosity. The other stuff is obvious junk that goes in the garbage can. **You have to survive the initial sort.**

To make matters more difficult, some people have a gatekeeper (if they're getting mail at work vs. home), but even at home someone's wife may throw away your letter if it looks like junk or it's obviously a solicitation. Surviving the sort is not an easy task and letters, no matter how fascinating or needed, are often thrown away, unopened.

If They Don't Read Your Masterpiece, What's the Point?

You just can't assume your mail will be opened and read.If you send out 100 letters this week, don't dare assume "I'm sending 100 letters and 100 people will read them".

If you're in a competitive area where 50 other attorneys are mailing the same person, all using white envelopes with the name of a law office on each,

Why would they ever open <u>your letter</u>?

The most extreme example I've seen of this is in Los Angeles. There are literally 100 different attorneys direct mailing for criminal cases. There are guys doing really well but believe me, they're NOT not just sending run-of-the-mill white envelopes. There's a lot more to direct mail than meets the eye.

You have to go out of your way to differentiate what you send to ensure direct mail works for you.

How can you increase the likelihood someone is going to open and read your mail? Try using "grabbers" –

small items you put into your mail piece that give it a 3D effect.

For instance, I've used a small bag of shredded money, a compass, a little toy soldier, a rock, and all kinds of small objects to make the mail I send out **lumpy**.

When someone gets an envelope that's bulging with an object inside, natural curiosity will lead them to open and read it. And that's the whole point.

Get your mail OPENED and then READ.

Don't just throw something weird inside but tie it into your letter itself.

Let's say throw in a miniature hourglass (30 cents each) and reference the object in your letter by saying, "Time may be running out on your criminal case."

You're referencing the grabber, the envelope is lumpy and 3D, and the whole package makes sense to the recipient. It may even make them smile.

A higher open rate, curiosity, and a unique angle will improve your direct mail results dramatically.

Another way to differentiate your mail is to hand-write on the envelope, or put testimonials in with your letter. You can send an oversized envelope, or send by tube mailer.

Did you know you can literally mail a 6" tall big pill bottle or a bank bag? Imagine potential clients getting a zippered, canvas purse you'd normally put money in and take to the bank with your letter inside or a gigantic pill bottle, with your prescription for legal help inside.

I bet you'll get nearly 100% of people to open it.

Do you know what happens when someone gets these items in the mail? They look at it and think, "What the heck is this thing and who sent me **THIS?**"…

…and they OPEN IT. Now you've got a fighting chance for them to read it and call you.

Direct mail DOES work. Don't be afraid of trying unusual mailings like my suggestions here. It's worth the small extra expense to get far more readership, calls and CLIENTS.

Don't let "cost" hold you back.

The only thing that matters is ROI. (Return on investment).

Suppose you spend $1 per person for your boring, "me-too" white envelope mailer:

Results: You spend $2,000 a month in direct mail at $1 per letter mailed (2,000 letters sent). 1 in 100 people call, and 1 in 4 calls retain you. At $1 per mailer, you're paying $100 to get a phone call and $400 to get a retained client. An average client pays $1,000 retainer.

Your ROI is: ($1,000 * 5 clients) / $2,000 spent = 250%

Expensive? Let's compare.

<u>**Scenario 2:**</u> You wipe away your tears and fears, and use a pill bottle with letter inside, and spend $2,000 a month, but this time, at ***$3.50 per mailer***, you send out only 571 letters vs. 2,000 letters.

This time, 1 in 20 people call you, and 1 in 4 retain.

You retain 7 clients (rounding down) at $1,000 each, making your ROI: ($1,000 * 7 clients) / ($2,000 spent) = 350%.

Which one is more "expensive?"
Which one is more effective?

Would you rather spend $2,000 to get $5,000,
or spend $2,000 to get $7,000? ☺

Doubts About Direct Mail -Dispelling Misconceptions

Direct Mail sounds great, but is greatly feared by attorneys.

"My State Bar won't allow me to do that."

Have you checked on the actual rules in your state?

Many states DO allow direct mail, as long as it satisfies some easy State Bar requirements regarding disclosures, and disclaimers.

Some of the common rules I've seen is it has to say "Attorney Advertisement" in a certain large font at the top of the letter. No problem. Be compliant, but don't be afraid.

Another common rule requires the disclaimer: "If you've already found legal counsel, please disregard this letter." No problem; you can write that. Don't assume, "I can't do it."

Have you heard this misconception? - "Direct mail only gets you crappy clients with no money, or tire kickers."

Not true. You can get some really good clients from direct mail if you're mailing for DUI or other specific offenses.

If you're only mailing for traffic tickets, well then what do you expect to get?

Some of my attorney clients have gotten $10,000 cases from direct mail. Assuming will only make you miss out on this opportunity to get clients.

Assumptions can cripple you:

"People don't read nowadays. It's all internet-based."

Interested people DO read compelling and relevant information that helps them.

When they get a well-written direct mail piece that is relevant to them, you would be surprised who comes out of the woodwork and calls you to retain. It's all walks of life; believe me.

"Direct mail doesn't work. I've tried it before;"

"There's too much competition."

Yes, in some major metros, there IS A LOT of competition, but you can find a niche and succeed and profit from your spend. If you send a plain white envelope, a boring letter- and not split-test it and track it, not grabbers, different envelopes, stamps and testimonials- then sure – your competition will stomp all over you and you'll lose money.

However, if you work at it, direct mail is a very powerful way to get clients. I don't care how much competition there is. I did a mailer for an attorney in

Los Angeles, where there are literally 100 people competing and mailing, and he got plenty of responses and profited from the effort. If it can be done there, it can be done anywhere. Trust me.

"Direct mail is unprofessional;"

"I'm bothering people by sending them mail;"

Ok, starve to death then because you're assuming that people who respond to a letter in the mail don't really need help and would be "offended". Other guys who DO do direct mail will happily eat your lunch, dinner, and tomorrow's breakfast.

"What will other attorneys think of me?"

Do you really care? Do you think other attorneys' opinions have any bearing on whether you go broke, feed your family, or retained 10 clients last month vs. 2 the month before? Worry about yourself. Everyone else is busy doing the same thing - worrying about themselves.

Below the Radar and in the Dark

One cool thing about direct mail is it operates below the radar and in the dark. Unless another attorney sees your letter, or if a client has brought it in for some reason, most attorneys have no idea what you're doing in direct mail. Sure, they'll start to see you in court a lot and wonder what your secret is, but that makes it all the better, doesn't it?

On the internet where everything you do ends up on YouTube, Facebook or Google Search Results. On the internet, everything can be copied at light speed.

Direct mail is success through stealth.

If Referrals Are The Best Clients, Why Aren't You Focused On Getting More of them? (Newsletters to Past Clients)

I'm sure you get referrals from past clients, yes? And when you do, I'd bet they're the best clients, not only because they are "free" to retain, but they're probably the best behaved clients as well. You don't have to do much work to convince them to retain you because they're **"pre-sold".**

I'm sure you smile to yourself when someone calls and says, "My friend / neighbor / father / mother / cousin / whoever referred me to you."

Referrals are the best kind of clientbecause they're less resistant to price; they're more willing to work with you and have less resistance to what you tell them.

So if referrals are so good, why aren't you focusing on getting more of them?

Here's the voices inside many attorney's heads when asked about generating more referrals:

"If I ask my past clients to refer me, I'm bothering them.
I already get referrals.
I'm not going to get anymore by bothering these people."

If done properly, this won't be true in the least.

Yes, I understand that if you're a criminal defense attorney, your past clients hope never to hear from you again…

…but what they are actually hoping to never hear about is their past criminal case.

Your past clients have now moved on with their lives, but they're certainly okay to hear about general topics of interest they may enjoy in their normal life.

We'll get into how you can communicate with them on topics that are outside the law - instead about things they enjoy. **Then they won't mind** hearing your name again and again; especially if you got positive results in their case and you have interesting, useful info to impart to them.

Why Focus On Getting Referrals? Is it Worth It?

You're probably already spending thousands a month on Yellow Pages, SEO, Google pay-per-click, direct mail, TV, radio, billboards, Facebook, Twitter, or some other marketing fad of the day.

It's time to redirect a tiny portion of that money to getting more referrals.

Before I explain HOW, check out the story of a vehicle accident attorney from Vancouver Canada who gets 77% of all his new clients from past client referrals.

This blew me away when I heard it, and I couldn't believe it.

What this guy does is send a paper and ink, physical monthly newsletter to all his past clients. He's been doing this for years, and told me it really doesn't cost all that much.

Over the years he adds past clients to the list, and he swore he gets plenty of calls from these people. People even call to say: "I love your newsletter. It's interesting. My friend Joe was in a car accident and I thought of you, so I told him to call you."

With 77% of his business coming from past client referrals, this attorney is pretty happy, because he doesn't need to blow thousands on various marketing efforts.

He already has a great resource of people sending him clients. It's fantastic and definitely do-able if you work at it.

Here's how you can copy his success: Send all your past clients a monthly printed newsletter by post office mail; **not just email.** It has to be a physical, paper and ink mailer sent once a month; not every 6 months or once a year.

If this sounds daunting, let me make it a little easier for you.

Start with your most recent past clients until you reach ones that have been gone for up to 2 years. Why? Because up until 2 years, many people are still living at the same address.

2 years of past clients will give you enough of a starting base that you can contact a fair number of them successfully. The average solo practitioner I've seen gets about 85 clients a year. If you take the past two years, you have a solid base of 170+ past clients to work from.

So how much does it cost to keep your name in front of these people? Let's say you have 200 names; the average cost to send a newsletter is $1.50 / person / month, including postage. Spend $300 per month to **communicate 12x a year with 200 of your past, happy clients? It's a no brainer.**

To keep your list clean and effective, make sure to add new clients as you complete their cases, and remove ones that no longer have valid addresses or come back as returns.

Let's look at the numbers. $300 a month x 12 = $3,600 a year to mail to your list. One referral case every 3 months,
(at $1,200 a case) means you'll at least break even.

Keep up your mailer consistently, and you'll retain quite a bit more than that as your newsletters' visibility and stickiness in peoples' memories improves.

It's a cost effective way to keep in contact with your list, keep your name in front of them, and get referrals. It pays for itself pretty darn quick and makes you money.

Why and how does a monthly newsletter to past clients work?

Your past client, John Smith, is not an orphan. He might have a wife and kids. Maybe his parents are alive and he has sisters, brothers, cousins, people at work and people he knows in his social circles through Facebook.

Let's say you represented John Smith a year ago on a DUI case, and you got his charges reduced, helped him avoid jail, and he's happy with your legal representation.

Now John starts getting your monthly newsletter; and at first, nothing happens. After 3 months of getting your newsletter, he's used to getting and seeing it come in the mail. He's even glanced through it a couple of times, and your name comes to mind when he gets the mail, thinking, "Huh. There's Attorney X's monthly mailer. Cool."

Nothing happens, but after about 4 months of getting your newsletter, John's cousin, Joe Blow, gets into a fight with his girlfriend. The fight gets loud and police are called.

Joe Blow is arrested and charged with domestic violence. He is freaking out and ends up on John's couch because there is an order of protection and he can't go home.

Joe: *"Man what am I going to do? You know any lawyers I can talk to?"*

<u>John:</u> *"Remember my DUI a while back? My guy XYZ helped me out. He sends me this letter in the mail each month and it's got his name on it. Let me look… Ok, here it is. Call him, he can help you out like he did for me."*

Voila! Joe Blow calls you as a referral. Without that paper newsletter, your past client might've easily said, "I had this guy who helped me out, but I don't remember his name. I…uh… think it was… Never mind. Just Google it and you'll get someone."

Which situation is going to get you business without you having to go hunting for it? Would you rather have your name in front of your past clients or have them forget about you, which, **believe me**, happens all the time.

➔ A monthly newsletter to past clients **<u>works</u>**.

What should your newsletter contain? Remember, it is not going to be about legal issues, because people don't want to hear about that scary stuff.

I know you're extremely busy, in court, dealing with all kinds of issues, preparing for trial, and the idea of writing a whole newsletter each month and sending it out yourself ***"ain't gonna happen"***- I get it.

Don't worry – I havea an easy way where you don't have to write a single word. You don't even have to mail it out yourself. There are automated solutions, and templates with all the articles you need in them.

If you don't have time, you can get a professional looking, informative and interesting newsletter out the door monthly with zero effort on your part.

No Work? Let me explain how it's possible

Instead of a boring, law-filled, scary newsletter, the key is to make it a mini-Reader's Digest format.I have access to multiple services that provide a template of articles that change monthly, including things like a recipe from a famous cook, a crossword puzzle, Sudoku or word jumble.

Also included will be several articles about current events, a celebrity, and a historical figure. Also included is an article about what's going on this month. (ex: February is Black History Month, so the newsletter template would contain an article on a famous black person in history)

It WOULD be ideal if there was at least 1 article that talked about you and things in your personal life you're willing to disclose.

Let's say you're an avid golfer, you may want to include an article this monthabout your golfing experiences. Next month an article about your son's baseball team success. The month after that, a trip you took your family on to Disney.

Even with 1 personal article, your newsletter is still 90% template. At worst, you may want to carve out 15 minutes a month to personalize your newsletter further with an article.

The initial setup is where all the work comes in, and it's barely 30 min of work: You want to have your law firm's name, your name, your picture, address, phone#, email, and a short call to action:

> ***"Call me anytime for legal help. I'm ready to step in and help you again as I've helped you in the past."***

Why would anyone waste their time reading MY newsletter?

Millions of people read and subscribe to the Reader's Digest. My wife subscribes, and I've found myself sitting in the bathroom, reading an article or two… It has human interest stories, tips on saving money, surprising research, a crossword, and all kinds of generically appealing stuff.

I enjoy getting it; so do millions of people over the past 50 years, and if your newsletter is similar, guess what?

Your past clients will read and enjoy it.

The newsletter, done right, has mass appeal. It's not pushy - It's informative, interesting, non-threatening, entertaining, and **<u>IT GETS READ</u>**.

Unbeknownst to your past clients, it's secret missionis to keep your name in front of your past clients without boring or scaring them with legal issues.

Sadly, although it's a brain dead simple process nowadays, and totally automated, most attorneys are unwilling or afraid to do these newsletters. ..

<u>Here are some lame excuses I've heard:</u>

1. **"It costs too much"** $1.50 per month per person is ridiculously cheap; there is no cheaper form of communication than that.

   Your mailer is 100% targeted, and is highly effective. The ROI can be off the charts, and it blows away any result you'd ever get from generic ads in magazines, newspapers, pay per click, or website visitors.

2. **"I don't have time"** Even if you don't want to write a single word, there are services that can help. I'll even help you set up the newsletter the first time or you can use a provider that will do it for you.

For a pathetically small fee of about $80 a month, many services will populate the newsletter with new, current, topical articles each month.

You don't even have to mail it out – a newsletter service will even do THAT for you. Push a button, and out it goes.

3. "It's a lot of work to get my past client list together." Have your admin do it. Maybe she'll curse your name for a few days, but once it's done, it's done.

Now you're off to the races. Every time you get a new client, just add them to the list. If you get 10 new clients a month, it will take you 1 minute each client to add them to your list. (10/month * 12 = 120 additional subscribers)

4. **"I don't know what to write"** Again, there are "done for you" solutions. You don't have to write.

5. **"No one's going to read this junk"** We talked about this. The Reader's Digest model works.

6. **"Can I just mail it once a year or every six months instead of every month?"** Once every six months or 1x a year isn't enough.

Stop being a cheapskate, and don't worry that you're "bothering people". You're NOT. Once a month is a sweet spot - rare enough that it doesn't harass the person, yet frequently enough so they remember you.

After someone's received and eyeballed 3, 4 or 5 newsletters, they know every month they'll get one from you and will actually **look forward to getting it**.

You'll stay in their minds, and it's highly likely there will be lingering copies sitting around the house. Being able to grab it and call, or hand it to a friend, co-worker, or family member in need beats sending someone to the Google jungle, only to be suckered away by competition.

7. **"I don't want to bother people"** Stats shows that well over 60% of people ***enjoy*** getting direct mail, unlike email, which is literally 94% SPAM.

   Getting something in the mail is like a gift. This gift, the newsletter, may be four pages back to front. It doesn't take long to read. All the content is enjoyable.
   You can read it on the toilet. You can sit for five minutes and read it. It works very well.

8. **"Can I just email it instead of going through the hassle of direct mailing it?"** You can, but SHOULD **NOT**. Direct mail is a lot more powerful than just email. Physically getting something in the mail, holding it in your hands, opening it, and sitting down and reading it makes it a one-on-one experience.

   You can't be distracted by the internet, Twitter or Facebook. You can't click to another web site. You can't lose the file on your computer. It sits around your house and you are reminded of it over and over. You will look at it and read it. Direct mail beats the piss out of email in response rates.

   With email deliverability rates these days, if you send an email to 1,000 people, only about 10% lately are really opening and reading it. 50% often don't even GET YOUR EMAIL because of spam filters. That is a good rate. Some are 5% or 1%. You may think a lot of people are reading your newsletter by email, but very few are. Direct mail works a lot better.

Even MORE Good Reasons to Send a Monthly Physical Newsletter

Did you know a paper newsletter is just like a news PAPER or MAGAZINE that you control? You can put a special offer in your newsletter, each month or every few months. How about offsetting the cost or even profiting from sending it out by advertising the legal practice of someone in a different practice area? (ex: You do DUI. They do divorce.)

Why not sell cheap advertising space to a dentist, chiropractor, tax prep person or estate planner? These people can totally offset the cost of your mailing by paying you to advertise in your mailer.

Tell a dentist you mail to 400 people once a month. Charge them $99 a month to put an ad in for dentistry. How's THAT for cheap, effective advertising?

Newsletters are cheap, effective and an excellent way of mining your old client list; clients you mistakenly thought were dead, gone and unable to help you can make you a LOT more money than you ever imagined.

Surviving the Google Pay Per Click Strip Club with Your Wallet Intact

Everyone has either heard of or tried Google pay-per-click (PPC)(Aka Google Adwords). No, not paperclips you use to hold paper together, but pay-per-click, like you does with a mouse. Click, click, and click.

Watch out, because Google Pay-per-click service can empty your wallet faster than any strip club ever could, leaving you "frustrated" all the same.

Most attorneys that try it get burned pretty quickly. It's alluring, to be sure, because PPC promises immediate clicks, calls, clients, and floods of traffic. That is how it's sold; but it is a very dangerous, expensive, competitive arena to play in. I'm here to tell you what to do so you don't get burned, and limp away thinking, "Google Adwords doesn't work".

First of all, you're probably going to shy away from its complexity and hire a 'Google-Certified PPC Firm'. Bad, bad move 90% of the time. Why?

Nearly all the PPC firms I've worked with use THEIR account to run your adwords campaigns, not YOUR OWN ACCOUNT. This means you're going to get filtered, useless information through a 3rd party that's unverifiable.

You say you don't care, you just want the phone to ring?

Good luck there, buddy. Without a way to track your PPC spending and match it with phone calls or contact form submissions on your website, you're begging to be taken for a ride twice - once by the PPC provider, and again by Google itself.

Did you also know that your "budget" (let's say $1,500 a month) gets allocated partly to pay the PPC company and partly to advertise for clicks? How much actually goes towards paying for clicks? You'll never know. Could be 80%, could easily be 30% - it's often 50% or less.

No reason on earth you can't have your own PPC account, provide the login and password to a PPC provider, and have them run it for you...

"Sir, that's not how we do things at XYZ Adwords Company. Don't worry, our proprietary, bullshit dashboard will show you this and that, and blow smoke up your ass... I mean, uh, show you floods of traffic and all the calls you're getting from advertising."

You hear this crap, don't hire the company. Anyone that can't use YOUR account, so you can login anytime and verify 1st hand what's going on is playing you for a sucker.

Typical rates for REAL PPC companies that actually know what they're doing are 20% of spend, and you pay them separately from your spend / budget.

How Complicated IS Google Adwords?

Google pay-per-click looks really simple, but is extremely complicated, just like trying to fly a 747 Jet Plane.

Hundreds of controls, levers, dials, specifications possible:

- You can choose to advertise in a certain geographic area, (ex: an 8-mile radius around your office)
- You can choose different keywords. Let's say you're in Atlanta, Georgia. You can chooseas keywords:
  - "Atlanta Personal Injury Lawyer," "Discount Atlanta Personal Injury Attorney" "Atlanta DUI Lawyer" or "Best Atlanta Sex Crimes Attorney." Should you bid on a few keywords or hundreds? Which ones?
- How much will you pay to bid on a keyword? Will you pay more on some vs. others?
- What times of day will you advertise? 24/7? Just office hours? Only Sunday thru Tuesday, 7am-7pm?
- Do you know what negative keywords you're going to start out with? (keywords that trigger your ads NOT to show up. Ex: "free" "cheap" "pro bono")
- Will your ads show on laptops, smartphones, ipads, or just desktops?
- How many different ads are you going to test? Which ad goes with which keyword? How will you know if an ad is "better" than a different ad?

- Do you know how to track and tie a click on your ad to an actual phone call or contact form filled in?
- Where will your ad appear on the page? Bottom or top? How much will you have to pay per click to get a certain position on the page?
- Troubleshooting: Google PPC is a fickle beast - malfunctions ALL THE TIME. Things don't work as planned - do you know how to diagnose what's going on and fix it?
- How much is your daily and monthly budget? How many clicks will it take to get someone to call or email on average?
- How much do you have to spend to retain a client, on average? Is that number $400? Is it $3,000? Is that 'expensive' or 'worth it'? Does it bring you ROI?
- How much does it cost to get a click? Is your market $10 a click or is it $20 a click? Can you even begin to afford that?

Is that complex enough for you? Do you have the time to even scratch the surface and put together a campaign that will make sense, not rob you blind and return you nothing, and actually **make you money**?

Welcome to the Google Adwords Strip Club, where daily ad spend budgets, to even be let in the door, typically run $50 - $100 a day, which translates to $1,500 - $3,000 a month.

A lot of markets, such as DUI or criminal defense are horrifically expensive, running $8, $15, $30, even $40 a click.

A daily budget of $100 can easily be eaten up with a meager 10 clicks or less. I've seen it happen many times.

Some major metros have such competitive, rabid markets, you could blow $100 by 10am and miss out on all the traffic later in the day.

Your monthly budget could easily run out the first week, and then you have no more money for the month. This is a serious game for serious players and requires extensive knowledge to run properly.

Don't Just Sit There, Helpless-How to Run Google PPC the Right Way & Figure Out if It's Profitable or Garbage

Instead of terrifying you with all the complications of Google Adwords, I'll give you some insight into how to run a successful campaign with a hope of making money… OR, figure out quickly that this form of advertising is NOT working for you and quit before you go broke.

In Google PPC, the ads you write are one of the biggest drivers of success vs. failure.Typical, me-too ads that say that same junk as everyone else: "We'll fight for you," "Call today," "24-hour free consultation" will get lost in the noise and do nothing for you.

In other advertising mediums, this means mediocre results, but in Google Adwords, this will get you absolutely nowhere.

Google is a harsh mistress, and punishes crappy advertisers with higher pay per click prices, low traffic, and no profit if you don't have compelling ads that get clicked on more than your competitions' ads.

Think Google cares about your money? Not a bit. They make in the neighborhood of $40 BILLION a year, and you're a cockroach to be stepped on, not catered to.

Google's mission is to provide the most relevant search results to people Googling stuff. It's the most competitive ad space on planet Earth. Punishing you with higher costs that drive you out is a part of the game - there are tons of other advertisers you're competing against.

Their theory is a good ad serves their customers better and attracts more clicks. Coincidentally, clicks always cost more in the beginning because you building an account history that Googles' computers and technicians are evaluating.

Anyway, the ad itself is critical. The right ad can make you money and the wrong ad can lose you money. So you have to come up with ethical, creative ads that address, within a microsecond, what people are looking for. It's not an easy thing to do.

Typical *'click through rates' are a measly 1%* (ratio of # of times your ad appears in search vs. the # of people that clicked). Once someone clicks on your ad, they come to a "landing page" - a certain page on your website. (99% of attorneys send clickers to their homepage).

Let's say your law practice does criminal defense, DUI and car accidents. Also, you have 3different attorneys at your firm, each of whom handles a different area of law.

Sending someone that clicked on a DUI ad to a homepage with 3 different practice areas is more distracting than helpful.

You want to send people to a custom page that immediately addresses what they clicked on. If they clicked on a DUI ad, send them to a DUI-specific page.

If they click on a car accident ad, send them to a page on car accidents. You can get even more specific than that. Let's say you're targeting 1st time DUI offenders. Instead of sending clickers to a generic DUI page, best to send them to a "what you must know about 1st time DUI" page, right?

The more specific you make your whole sales process using Google Adwords, the better your results are going to be.

Remember, customers go through a progression of "googling something", eyeballing ads, clicking on a compelling one, landing on a relevant or non-relevant page, then either engaging, reading and calling you, or clicking the back button and wasting your money and their time… on to a million other competitor websites they go!

How to Choose a Worthwhile Google PPC Management Company and Not Get Burned

Most Google PPC companys' jobs are to take your money and keep you in the dark. Never, ever, ever, ever use anything but your own Google Adwords account that you provide access to.

Here's what to ask:

First say, "I am going to give you access to my pay-per-click account. I don't want your pay-per-click account. You use mine." If they won't do this, walk away. You want to own the account, and provide access. Make sure you can lock them out if they don't do their job at 10pm the night before you call and fire them by changing your account password.

- Do you split test ads? Do you write different ad copy? How often will you change my ads up?
- What keywords are you proposing to bid on?
- What negative keywords are you going to use?
- What geography, times of day, and days of week do you propose for best results?
- How much are your fees? (standard is 20% of spend)
- What do you suggest for my budget and why?
- What's the average cost per click for my chosen markets?
- Do you provide month to month service or require a long-term contract? (it WILL take 30-60 days to test and ramp up a campaign, but never sign more than a 6 month agreement - no reason to do it at all)
- Do you create and split test landing pages? Do you even know what a freakin' landing page is?
- Do you know what broad, phrase, or exact match is?
- Do you set up conversion tracking? (a conversion is a phone call or a contact form filled out) (can you tie back a specific keyword to the ad that was clicked to the phone call that was generated?)
- Are you Google Certified? (meaningless, but ask anyway)
- Have you worked on attorney PPC campaigns before, specifically in my practice areas?
- Will you tell me if pay-per-click is just not working for me? (Yeah, good luck getting someone you pay to tell you it is not working for you - might as well ask to freak them out)

Honestly, I would actually look for a full-fledged marketing consulting company; not just a pay-per-click only company.

You want someone that does SEO, pay-per-click, direct mail, newsletters; the whole boat - someone that specializes in attorney marketing.

Why?

A multi-faceted, attorney specialist marketing company is **incentivized to say**, "All right, we tried pay-per-click. It didn't work. Let's move on to something else that will work." They're not married to pay-per-click, nor are they a one-trick pony where if pay-per-click doesn't work, they have nothing else to offer except being fired. A pay per click only company will never, ever tell you that Adwords isn't working - it's against their interest to do so.

Yes, Google Adwords CAN WORK. It's not impossible, it's actually quite do-able and potentially profitable… IF you get experienced help and know at least the basics of how it works.

Fact: Google Adwords essentially requires a $2,000+ tuition to be paid before you can expect profitable results. Sad, but true.

And don't think that you'll ever get anywhere with Google Adwords if you don't track phone and web contact form conversions. Might as well throw your money out the window at 60 mph.

You know what? Google PPC is worse than paying strippers for lap dances. At least you're happy for an hour or so, before you leave frustrated.

PRICING YOUR SERVICES WITHOUTCUTTING YOUR OWN THROAT

Pricing your services is a huge issue, especially in the bad economy of the past six years.

I've done studies and I can tell you prices vary drastically not only by the metro area, but by the attorney themselves!

In your city, at this very moment, there are DUI attorneys charging $750, while right down the street, others are charging $3,000.

Both of these guys co-exist in the same city.

They see the same potential audience of clients.

Some lawyers are starving to death, and some gross $500,000 a year. There's a LOT that needs to be said about price and pricing your services without cutting your own throat.

First of all: **never be the lowest cost attorney. Ever.**

I think you already know that, deep down inside.Yes, there's a lot of pressure from competition squawking low prices and $500 down to start your case. The economy sucks. Potential clients beat you up on price and the entire world seems to be on a payment plan.

Trust me, bad advertising is everywhere, and there are plenty of attorneys in your market that will sooner kill it vs. make any money, offering DUI's starting at $750, Bankruptcies for $400 down, or all misdemeanors starting at $1,500. Ignore their advertising because they will go into a death spiral and drag you down with them if you let yourself be swayed.

No one can do a good job, working for a pauper'swage.

When you talk to potential clients, you have to be prepared to defend your price.You know, better than I do, that this "elephant in the room" is permanently parked there, just waiting to be recognized, at each and every consultation.

Let's say you charge $3,000 for a 1st time DUI case with no trial anticipated, and competition is quoting $1,500.

Potential clients can't help but think, "Attorney XYZ only charges $1,500, and this guy (you) is quoting me $3,000. Is it really worth it to spend that extra money?"

Even if they don't voice this concern, it's on their mind. You've gottaaddress it, defend against it, prepare your case for the 'price jury' and be ready, just like a court case. If you don't have a prepared statement or set of statements you can use anytime you talk to a potential client to justify your price, you're asking for trouble.

Easy to say, but hard to do: How DO you defend price or make it a non-issue before it's dark spectre is raised?

One way I've seen "A"-level marketers use, (which I think is fantastic), is to first build up the value of your services to 3, 5, or 10x what you're asking a client to pay. You show clients that number; then you discount way down and show them your final number.

I go into this strategy in a lot more depth shortly, (also, see attached sample worksheet)but for now, that's the basic structure.

Remember, you're not just justifying your price, you're also battling "private attorney vs. public defender vs. no attorney".

Do you have a prepared and compelling arugment why it's a horrible idea for potential clients to defend themselves?

Why should someone hire you vs. use a public defender or look for legal aid services?

How about hiring your competition vs. you? What makes YOU so special?

Typical arguments aren't going to cut it, especially in todays highly competitive, zero attention span, marketed-to-by everybody world potential clients live in.

"You get what you pay for."
"I'm not the cheapest in town."
"I'm aggressive."
"I care about my clients."

Not very compelling. I'm sorry, but that's boilerplate.

How about:
"I deliberately limit the number of clients I take. This allows me to spend a lot of personal time on your case. I can delve way deep into the issues and find every possible defense to your case, to the point of overkill."

"I'll attend every court date - no junior associates here that suddenly appear in court with your file in hand and no personal knowledge of your case."

"I'll never just throw you under the bus to get you sign a plea agreement. Only after we've exhausted every possible alternative will we plea your case out."

“I charge what I feel is a reasonable rate, especially since the alternative of losing costs 5x more than I charge.”

“I’ve overseen 700+ cases. The judges, prosecutors, and court personnel know me, and I know how the local courts function and their peculiarities. I know which judges tend to rule this way vs. that. Which prosecutors tend to agree to this vs that. We have a mutual respect for each other, and that benefits you tremendously in court.”

If you make a compelling offer to a potential client, you just may avoid the money excuses that clients give, and cut off peoples’ reservations before they voice them or leave your office, never to return.

Many potential clients won’t even tell you that they think you’re too expensive, but they’ll think it if you don’t make preparations, and they won’t hire you because of it.

If a potential client says, “You're too expensive;” or “That's a lot of money;” or “I don't have any money.”, or “I don’t have enough money.”, it’s often because you haven’t prepared them sufficiently and allayed their fears that they’re making not only the best choice, but the obvious and ONLY choice that will get them the result they desperately need.

Statements like these are a defense mechanism, and often don't mean they don't have money. Take notice of when you hear protestations about price. In what situation are you hearing them? What was your conversation like?

The way you talk to clients in person, through email, text message, and on the phone is very important and either sways them towards or away from you. Show them so much value that ***you are the clear choice to hire***, vs. everyone else in your market.

The better you are at preparing for and defusing pricing objections, the more potentials you'll retain, the more selective you'll become, and best of all? You can charge a heck of a lot more, have fewer clients, make the same or greater money, be the envy of your fellow attorney brethren.

Read on for a specific example how to present your value and subsequent price, based on marketing gurus' best practices:

A Neat Way to Combat, "I Have No Money", "You're Too Expensive", or "I Can't Afford It"

Why: "I don't have any money;" "I don't have enough money" or "You're too expensive." no longer have to derail your retention process.

You spend time, effort and serious money just to get potential clients to agree to and show up for an initial in-office consultation. On average, smart lawyers like you spend $600-$1,000 in marketing, staff time, and your time, just to get someone in the door?

Sadly, at the end of an initial consultation (that cost you so dearly just to get) you run into pricing issues, and many times, have no good defense on how to keep your prices high enough to earn a good return.

I surveyed 38 attorneys on what they do to combat pricing objections like these. Pricing pressure is pretty pervasive (PPPP) and can put your law practice into a death spiral quickly.

Of course you don't want to take on clients that truly have no money. Initial upfront screening can help dramatically, however, when potential clients say, "I don't enough money;" "You're too expensive" or "I don't have any money," many times it is because you haven't built enough trust or value to differentiate yourself as the OBVIOUS CHOICE when shopping attorneys for their case.

The trick is to build trust, rapport, likeability, and authority in a prospect's mind BEFORE you reveal your price.If you've sufficiently built up enough value, when you reveal your price, hiring YOU will be cheap in comparison to any and every other alternative.

Top marketing gurus go through this exact flow when pitching people to buy their products, so you can learn a lot from studying them as I have.

By going to a lot of marketing seminars, getting pitched by the best in the world, and coughing up $1,000-$3,000, I discovered their secrets that you can use in your own law practice to retain more clients, while charging premium prices. The way they pitch is always the same, but it works.

See the document on the next page which talks about the total cost of a DUI conviction? Let's go through it and I'll show you how to build value in the eyes of clients.

Attorney Marketing Association

Report of findings: Total cost of a DUI / DWI Conviction
(1st offense; national average; non aggravated; low BAC .08-.15)

Initial Vehicle Tow & Impound	$250
Bail Bond fees (if applicable; 10% of bond amt)	$250
Transport from Jail	$50
Request to Dispute Administrative Hearing (re: Driver License Suspension)	$110
Court Fees, Fines, Penalties	$1,250
Court Fee for Pleading Guilty	$250
Driver's License Suspension (avg 180 days) & Alternate Transportation Cost (taxi, bus) (avg $17 / day * 5 days/wk * 24 weeks)	$3,060
Increased Auto Insurance Premiums (avg 3 yrs of $116 / month increase)	$4,176
Driver's License Reinstatement Fees After Suspension is Completed	$375
Probation Costs ($250/mo * 12 months avg)	$3,000
Decreased Earning Ability Due to Criminal Conviction w/ avg 10 year Expungement if available ($10,000 a year * 10 years)	$100,000 ???
Expungement of Criminal Record (if available)	$1,500 ???

Total National Average Cost Estimate (Source: AMA) **$12,771**
(1st offense; non-aggravated; low blood alcohol level .08 - .15)

Bankrate.com's Total Cost of a DUI Calculation: $9,000 - $24,000
http://www.bankrate.com/finance/personal-finance/dui-memorial-day-20-000-1.aspx

MSNBC Money Magazine's Total Cost of a DUI Calculation: $10,000
http://money.msn.com/auto-insurance/dui-the-10000-dollar-ride-home.aspx

With a potential client, take this sheet out at the end of your consult or even in the beginning, depending how you want to structure your pitch.

The end results will be that by demonstrating that your price is much lower **than the price they would *have to***

pay if convicted. No, you can't guarantee an outcome, but a sure loser bet is far worse than a decent likelihood of mitigating their charges and circumstances.

When you step a potential client through the sheet above, they'll perceive your services in a totally different way. They'll no longer think you're "expensive". They won't think, "I don't have money." They'll realize, "I have GOT TO get money to hire this attorney to defend me because it's OBVIOUS that what he offers has 2, 3, or 5x the value of being convicted. In fact, I'm saving money by hiring him, not spending."

(your local grocery store uses "saving vs. spending"language, and now you know why)

I recommend introducing this document both at the beginning of some consultations and at the end of others, to test which is more effective. Your admin can step through the document if you're uncomfortable or unwilling to do it. Some attorneys do have their admins talk prices so clients won't perceive them as the bad guy - the secretary is the bad guy instead.

Now here's what you need to do:Pull out this document and say, "I want to show you a comparison of costs for pleading guilty or defending yourself vs. hiring a private attorney with years of experience like me.You'll be shocked at the price difference."

Now go through each of the line items, one by one to arrive at the bottom price. As you step through the items, ask: "Does this make sense to you?" Get them to agree to the potential cost of each item, and they'll readily agree to the bottom line number.

At the bottom, point to the number the red arrow points to - even circle it with a red pen for effect. Now look at the references below it.

Then say, "Here are 3 references from 3 neutral third parties showing total cost of a DUI conviction (adapt this document for any particular crime!) A reasonable person would certainly agree that I could charge that amount but personally, I think that would be ridiculous. My job is to get you results without draining your bank account."

Now put a big, red slash through that number and say, "I'm not going to charge you that amount. Heck, I'm not even going to charge you half that amount."

"For the work and time I'm going to put in defending your case, and to help you avoid paying this huge amount of money, I'm only going to charge you (a third or a quarter of that amount)." As you say this, write down your price.

"I may not be able to get your case thrown out or your charges reduced, but it's likely I can make a pretty serious dent, and help you avoid paying this huge number that you'd likely pay if you pled guilty, represented yourself, or had a public defender who doesn't have much time to spend on your case.

I'm stepping you through this document so you're fully informed **what you're getting &why I charge what I do.**

I think you see the tremendous value, bargain, and discount my fee asks, and people agree it's worth it in spades."

So that's the spiel. How do you think the potential client will perceive this? It works like magic and you've got to try it. What you're doing without saying it is starting with a much higher number that comes NOT FROM YOU, but from 3rd party, authoritative sources. The potential client becomes anchored to the $12,000 price that you're building up for them, step by step. You then step in to save the day, cross it out, and put your miniscule retainer fee in comparison.

NOW, when you need to take the discussion a step further if a payment plan is needed, for instance…

Write down your retainer fee; (ex: $2,500). "I'm not going to stop there. Because you're telling me money is tight, we can do just 2 payments of $1,250 (or 3 payments of $833)."

"You're getting $12,000 of value for an unbeatable price."

Building up the value, then coming back down to your retainer is going to cause a **very different reaction** in your prospect's mind vs. if you went through the whole consult, then just asked for your retainer at the end with no value build up first.

Don't be afraid to try this both at the beginning and at the end of your consultations, and let me know how much it boosts your retention rates and lowers price resistance.

To build up your value, you may want to have your admin go through this first, **before the potential even sees you for the consult**. Your admin can also do this at the end.

Utilize price strategy from the pros, like I did!

About The Author

Richard Jacobs is the author of two books:

- **"But I Only Had 2 Beers!"**
(Truth Talk from Over 25 DUI Lawyers)

- **Secrets of Attorney Marketing Law School Dares Not Teach**

Richard specializes in helping attorneys break free from 70 hour work weeks and marginal law practices, to help Attorneys nationwide transform their lives, bank accounts, and law practices into successful, revenue producing businesses.

Starting in 2009 with the growth of myDUIattorney.org from scratch into a nationwide force in providing advertising for DUI attorneys, Richard has helped hundreds of solo practitioners, 2, and 3 attorney small firms to learn, implement, and profit from sound marketing that law school dares not teach.

If you're ready to improve your law practice and break free of mediocrity & struggle, contact Richard today at Speakeasy Marketing, Inc.

20418541R00096

Made in the USA
Charleston, SC
12 July 2013